Dance Class

American High School Students Encounter Anthony Powell's
Dance to the Music of Time

Edited by

John A. Gould

Forward by Dr. Nicholas Birns, Eugene Lang College

iUniverse, Inc.
New York   Bloomington

Dance Class
American High School Students Encounter
Anthony Powell's Dance to the Music of Time

iUniverse books may be ordered through booksellers or by contacting:

iUniverse
1663 Liberty Drive
Bloomington, IN 47403
www.iuniverse.com
1-800-Authors (1-800-288-4677)

Because of the dynamic nature of the Internet, any Web addresses or links contained in this book may have changed since publication and may no longer be valid. The views expressed in this work are solely those of the author and do not necessarily reflect the views of the publisher, and the publisher hereby disclaims any responsibility for them.

ISBN: 978-1-4401-2903-2 (pbk)
ISBN: 978-1-4401-2904-9 (ebk)

Printed in the United States of America

iUniverse rev. date: 7/28/09

Gratefully, the editor would like to
dedicate this book to all the authors

All proceeds of *Dance Class*
will benefit the Anthony Powell Society.

CONTENTS

FORWARD

Dance for Everybody?
Teaching, and Living, Powell's Fiction

In 1964, Anthony Powell, in the course of what the U.S. Embassy in London denominated as "informal lectures to Ivy League colleges" stopped off, in the company of a friend, at Phillips Academy, Andover, a boarding school in Massachusetts. Among his observations was that the student writing showed evidence that the study of Latin was long since renounced. The essays by Andover students on Powell in this volume give inferential evidence that this is no longer the case. Their wide and precisely employed vocabulary indicates that some at least have studied Latin assiduously.

But this slight re-classicization, as it were, in U.S. student prose styles is not the point of this collection. The point is that there is a place in the world where the fiction of Anthony Powell has been taught regularly, That this is happening is laudable; that it should happen is necessary. Powell has always had a profusion of fans. But, though many of these are in academia, very few have taught Powell. Much of this has to do with the academics being likelier to be historians and classicists and social scientists and even paleontologists or mathematicians than teachers of modern literature; some of it has to do with the struggle of getting a still too little-known author into an already overcrowded canon; some of it has to do with the difficulty of teaching the long novel in an era when even specialists in Victorian studies feel self-conscious about teaching a long Victorian novel – a *Middlemarch*, a *Little Dorrit*, a *Vanity Fair* – to even talented college undergraduates. But still the effort must be made to teach Powell. Admirers of Powell's work often live in an artificial cocoon as to the popularity of "their" author. The people committed to Powell's work are so committed, as witnessed by the four or five prominent critics who mention his name in their writing at every conceivable opportunity, that we are apt to forget that it is teaching that keeps a book alive. All of the books deemed literary classics are so largely because they are taught as such. Kept with a milieu of fans, *Dance* will wither on the vine. Taught to students who can transmit their knowledge forward, *Dance* will live, as it deserves to live.

Gould challenged this last difficulty by proudly labeling his course (solecistically) "the Longest Novel Ever Written." This had the merit of making an asset out of a liability. It also transcended the entire issue of putting *Dance* in context or finding a context for *Dance*. Free to concentrate on the novel itself Gould got down to the nitty-gritty of teaching. And nobody is a more ideal candidate to do this than Gould. John Gould knows literature inside out, has written literary fiction, memoir, grammar textbooks, and familiar essays, and has the intimacy with the written word that can only come from persistently teaching it and dwelling upon it. He is also one of Anthony Powell's most dedicated and reflective readers, and Gould's insight into Powell is evident not only in his own introduction but in the insights of all the students included who have been taught and nurtured by him.

As the essays reveal, the students are ordinary American kids with no especial access to Powell's world. They are as at sea as most Americans would be to the idiolects of the British aristocracy, military, and educational system. And the great delight of these essays is these students read Powell without any preconceptions. Freshly regarding the work, they see Powell's world as it is, not as it is so often characterized to be. And it is this straightforwardness, which should suggest to any high school teacher, at whatever level, in whatever milieu – even in say an inner-city public high school – that their students can learn from Powell. And to college teachers as well. On both levels, we have foreclosed options to our students by underestimating their intelligence and adaptability. As a later British cultural product (one connected to Powell through Constant and Kit Lambert) put it, "the kids are alright." Seeing Powell through the eyes of this, students should make all of us who are teachers jettison whatever excuses or fears we have about not teaching them and proceed to offer our students access to the treasure Gould has unlocked for those fortunate enough to study with him. The distinguished Australian critic David McCooey, an admirer of Powell's, once said that *Dance* is not for everybody; Gould gives the strongest argument for the opposite point of view.

Part of the benefit for reading any texts with students is not teaching it to them, but having them teach it to you; better yet, having the entire class achieve a collective, pluralistic reading of a text. We see the results of this at the very beginning of *Dance Class* with Corey Simpson saying that Nick Jenkins "possesses an odd combination of accurate observation and wild imagination." The Jenkins family trust is compared by a student to his own – how Powell would have loved the practical applicability of a background complication mentioned *en passant*. Travis Pantin highlights what a failure Jenkins' seems at the end of *A Buyer's Market*, something important for understanding the narrative arc of the sequence. One wishes an adult critic would write a full-fledged article about the tolerance towards homosexuality so rightly pointed out by Mike Donelan, and so missed by people who would characterize Powell as a "conservative" in U.S. terms. Nathaniel Miller's delicious description of Erridge as "ironically executive" and Jimmy Yang's stress on the fundamental mystery about Jenkins's love for Jean Templer (given ballast by Luke Spears's parallel observations) crystallize insights that might have otherwise lain on the cusp of the Powell reader's awareness.

Thankfully, not all the papers are expository. We have pithy poems and mordant haiku, Matthew Cranney gives us a Gypsy's-eye view of the deflowering of Nick Jenkins, Alex Svec's hilarious pastiche of Julian Maclaren-Ross, William Koven's play on Matilda Wilson/Moreland/Donners, who might well have been a character better suited for an drama (or opera) than the novel-sequence in which she plays a minor role. Equally, not all the essays are "literary" – Jason Myung's decoding of the economic references in Widmerpool's speech, Kim Sugarman's primer on the "quota quickies," Nick Anschuetz's welcome briefing on Ezekiel 37, James

Seman's conspectus on the canals of Venice. Erica Blake on World War II in Ireland (a thumbnail sketch of a topic assayed at far greater length by Clair Wills's *That Neutral Island*). Nicole Lee's piece on Katyn pinpoints what this dark historical episode meant to Nick Jenkins, and to his creator. Foster Furcolo, the former governor of Massachusetts who wrote one of the first books about the Katyn Massacre, would be disappointed that a student in his state did not mention his book, But, as I also failed to do so in *Understanding Anthony Powell*, Governor Furcolo will have to forgive two of us in the afterlife. This weave of real life and fictional life, fact and whimsy, is what makes it so fascinating when a range of readers comment on the same book. For instance, Katherine Cascio's diagnosis of Dependent Personality Disorder in Maclintick might well have convinced General Conyers, had he met Maclintick and had he lived to the supercentenarian age his natural lifespan might well have given him.

Yet, despite the accomplishment and merit of every essay contained herein, this book is more than a collection of student work. Gould's introduction and notes also make it of use as an overall guide to Powell; this book can take its place on the shelf along with Spurling, Barber, and the various introductory critical books as a ready reference for the Powell fan and scholar. The cast of characters in each scene adds an element even Spurling does not provide, and reminds us that, if one takes at his word Powell's continual pronouncements that the sequence is one giant novel broken up into twelve individual books for the sake of convenience and the publishing industry, then the chapter actually becomes the key unit, in terms of narrative syntax, of the overall work.

And how better than to see the overall work plain than through young eyes? As Madeleine Fawcett says, "my dance continues." I write this as someone whose reading, and rereading, of Dance will always be irretrievably conditioned by the fact I first read it at age thirteen. How pleased I was to know what the Ada Leintwardine title *I Stopped at a Chemist* meant without having to wonder about it; figuring this out made me feel as if I had acquired the key to all hidden meanings. Though the experiences--literary and otherwise--of the first twenty years of life have a fullness and an intensity that subsequent ones cannot match, even those days characterized by what Wordsworth – not one of Powell's favorites, yet a poet he concedes was great – termed "the still, sad music of humanity" can gain from having experiences of great art associated with them. Gould, as he mentions, first read *Dance* in his twenties; we both know people who first read *Dance* in their seventies and are acute and gifted readers of the sequence. I am as happy to have first heard Khachaturian's Violin Concerto, as performed by David Oistraikh, at age 43 as I am to have read *Dance* at thirteen. But reading *Dance* so early will give these young women and men important gifts to have at their disposal throughout their lives, a gift that will never stop giving. They will have a stock of archetypes with which to associate acquaintances. When they have to talk about current politics as a way of breaking the social ice, they will reap the humor of the resemblance to uttering "It seems the nationalists have reached Peking" in 1928. They will learn how to deal unflappably with the wide range of preposterous situations, all the while facing melancholy ones with poise and resolution, having been partially made immune to the depredations of the world's Blackheads and Widmerpools and Pamelas and Murtlocks, and made receptive to the joys of the world's Stringhams, Morelands, Barnbys, and Umfravilles. *Dance* is a great work of literature; it is also a *vade mecum* to life. And part of the pleasure of reading these students' essays is knowing they will have it as such.

John Gould has put together a book full of ready reference for the reader of *Dance*; Anthony Powell put together a book that yields generously as a ready reference for human beings as they are conducted through time's steps. The reader should be heartily thankful for both achievements.

Nicholas Birns
November 29, 2008

INTRODUCTION

Why, exactly, is teaching literature a good idea? I became an English teacher over 40 years ago largely because I wanted to have a job that would let me keep my hands where my heart was – right there on the bookshelves, with all those works I had loved growing up. In 1970, having spent four years in front of English classes, I was introduced to Anthony Powell's comic epic-in-progress *Dance to the Music of Time* by a friend, and I read all of the then-nine volumes in nine straight days, a kind of Nick Jenkins orgy.

I never considered teaching the series, though, not even after the last volume was completed five years later. I was teaching high school students, after all, and how could I get a class to read 12 novels, all by the same writer, straight through? Still, as I began to consider bringing *Dance* into the high-school classroom, I could see so many advantages.

The massive text would challenge and expand the experience of the students. Few of them would already be aware of 20th-century British history – despite its chronological, geographical, and cultural proximity to their own world. They would have to discover what it was to be young amid the social whirls of Eton, Oxford, and London in the '20's; what the rise of Nazism felt like to those who were living within *blitzkrieg* range of Germany in the '30's and '40's; what patterns music, painting, writing, and the rest of the arts took during the first half of the century. Here is one reason to teach literature: it puts us in full relationship with worlds not our own.

Anthony Powell's writing would both challenge and reward the students, as well. It would take lots of discussion to unpack his prose. Take just one example:

> For some reason, the sight of snow descending on
> fire always makes me think of the ancient world –

legionaries in sheepskin warming themselves at a
brazier: mountain altars where offerings glow between
winter pillars; centaurs with torches cantering beside
a frozen sea – scattered, unco-ordinated shapes from
a fabulous past, infinitely removed from life; and
yet bringing with them memories of things real and
imagined, (QU 1-2)

Instantly we find ourselves discussing Greek and Roman
mythology, and we are led to its relationship to us, those
"memories of things real and imagined." We also must check the
meaning of *fabulous*, a word that means something very different
from its common use as an intensifier, as in, "Powell is a *fabulous*
writer." In short we become close readers of rich prose.

There's also the comedy of *Dance*'s language. We have to be
patient, but when it comes, it can weaken our knees. Whenever
Dicky Umfraville opens his mouth, get ready: "There was nothing
positive about Cosmo Flitton – barring, of course, his Wasserman
Test." (This line does require glossing "Wasserman Test.") Then
just a few lines later, Dicky remarks, "Harrison I liked in his way.
He mixed a refreshing cocktail of his own invention called Death
Comes for the Archbishop." (Gloss Willa Cather here.) So here
is a second reason to teach literature: to open up and explore the
myriad possibilities of language, its ability to make us laugh – or,
indeed, to weep. The last paragraph of *Hearing Secret Harmonies*
invariably moves me nearly to tears.

But for me, the real reason to study literature is to discover
our own humanity. It teaches us compassion because we must try
to understand the people that live between the covers of books.
There are more than 400 characters in *Dance*, and they range – as
Clint Eastwood might put it – from the good, to the bad, to the
ugly. Eventually we learn to care for them all – for Stringham,
for the Maclinticks (even the dreadful Audrey), for Bob Duport
(whom Nick would have us dislike), even (and God help us) for
Kenneth Widmerpool. Compassion is caring about the fates of

people even when we know everything about them; and consider this: only in literature is such knowledge possible.

During two different school years – 2002-3 and 2007-8 – I was given the opportunity to teach a senior elective at Phillips Academy, Andover, called "The Longest Novel Ever Written." For three trimesters students were invited to read *Dance*. As it comprises twelve novels, we would read four per term, beginning with *A Question of Upbringing* in September and arriving at last in June with *Hearing Secret Harmonies*. It would be a long voyage, I told them, but for many it would open their eyes, and it would be fun.

There was no commitment for signing on for the whole journey. A student would sign on for a trimester at a time, and there would be no shame in moving to another course partway through the year, although I was hoping that they would become captured by the first four books and stick on. About a third of them did; of the 23 that took the first term during the two years I taught it, twelve stayed on for the entire sequence. (A total of 33 students took the course for at least one term.) I couldn't blame the others for shifting; Andover has some extraordinary English electives; one boy, Luke Spears, left in the winter term to take a *Ulysses* seminar, but came back in the spring to finish up the final four books with us. (He was able to read books 5-8 on his own.)

For those who have not read the entire sequence, a brief summary may open the door: the narrator, Nicholas Jenkins, writes what is essentially a twelve-volume autobiography, though it focuses on much more about his friends than about himself. He covers the years 1921, when he is about 16 and a student at a school very much like Eton, to 1971, when he is living in the country very much like Somerset. There is one flashback to 1914 at the outset of World War I. In between, we follow Nick and his many friends and few antagonists through London's society and bohemia, World War II in Wales, Ireland, and London at MI-5 (Liaison), and the worlds of music, painting, and literature in post-war England. Dogging Nick's footsteps the entire way is Kenneth Widmerpool: a buffoon, a social climber, an apotheosis of ambition, a sexual curiosity, a tyrant – the word "villain" is utterly inadequate.

Nick's life is closely modeled on Powell's own, and some of the fun of investigating *Dance* is discovering how much he has relied on real-life figures in creating his characters. As I have suggested, much of the social, intellectual, economic, military, and political history of twentieth-century Britain is reflected in it as well. As a result, my students could find a wide range of historical questions raised in each book to investigate. Of course there were plenty of issues of literary criticism for them to spade through as well – the old favorites of plot, character, theme, and so on, as well as some technical questions growing out of writing such a long and sustained narrative.

Andover is a residential school, and the faculty has a good deal of freedom about how they set up their courses. I chose the three-class-meetings-a-week model, with two regular periods and one extended one. The longer I chose to conduct in my living room, following the example of the don Sillery. Instead of rock buns I served Dunkin Donut Munchkins, and we sat around on couches and chairs, hearing one of my colleagues describe his life as an undergraduate at Oxford, listening together to a tape of David Case reading the opening of *A Question of Upbringing*, or reading aloud and discussing the writing of Julian Maclaren-Ross, the model for X. Trapnel. By the by, on that latter occasion, I read them Maclaren-Ross's parody of Raymond Chandler, "So Long, My Buddy" from *The Funny Bone* (1956) – which inspired Alex Svec to write a marvelous parody of X. Trapnel, "Widmerpool's Private Eye," included here.

We read roughly a volume every two weeks. At the end of each, the students were asked to write a 3-4-page paper on any aspect of the novel that had interested them. We spent some time generating topics, but in the end the students were completely on their own. They were used to having English courses that required critical response, and most of them enjoyed discussing characters like Uncle Giles, J.G. Quiggin, and especially Widmerpool. Using the Oxford system of undergraduates' reading papers to a don, I asked each of them to read the paper aloud to me and to the rest of the class, and we then offered feedback before its final submission.

This process raised the caliber of papers significantly, but there was another element that pressured them to write well, which I employed with both classes. As each class moved through the sequence, I created a web site on which I published their papers. I also had them write a synopsis of each novel and a list of its significant characters. These web pages proved valuable for students that joined the class in the winter and spring terms, for they could refer to them to catch up with earlier events and characters without having to read the entire sequence. They also allowed students to refer to and build from their earlier work. Zach Smotherman wrote several essays about the influence of a military upbringing on Nick Jenkins's character. It even allowed Jimmy Yang, in his *Temporary Kings* paper, to cite Cassidy Carpenter's *Acceptance World* one. (All of these papers are included here.)

The most important effect of the web site was to introduce the students and their work to other readers of *Dance, viz.*, on-line members of the Anthony Powell Society. As I published each flight of papers, I alerted the Society's list-serve; a number of Powell aficionados sent back commentary on the essays. The students, in turn, quickly became aware that they were writing not just for me – their old LaBas – nor even for their classmates, but for a worldwide audience – and that audience was actually interested in what they were saying. One of the most wonderful moments of the year occurred when Nicole Lee cited an article by John Potter, a professor and scholar from Japan, who wrote back to us, thanking her for consulting his article. Nicole was delighted.

The Powell Society contributed in another way to "The Longest Novel Ever Written." At the end of the 2008 winter term, one of the members, Joan Williams, came to Andover from Toronto, and observed the presentations of the final papers of the trimester. And in June, another member, Eileen Kaufman, drove up from Connecticut to attend what was billed as an "Anthony

Powell Mini-Conference," joining me and other faculty members as the students read their *Hearing Secret Harmony* papers at a catered luncheon. This was a meeting fraught with significance: the end of the series, the end of their high-school careers (the Senior Prom – vaguely equivalent to the Huntercombes' ball – kicked off three hours after the festivities, putting a pinch on hairdressing time for some of the participants), and the end of my teaching career, as I retired right after that class. What else was left?

In deciding what this book should include, I thought that the synopses and character lists would be useful. First of all, they are a reflection of who and what the students found important as they read the novels. Secondly, they can be useful to someone reading an essay and needing a reminder of plot or character. I also have included a few extra items. The 2002 class wrote haiku, some of which I have set among an appropriate set of essays, and a couple of the Society's letters are here as well.

Finally, of course, are the essays themselves. They are arranged by novel so that someone that has just finished *The Kindly Ones*, say, can skip right to those. I have included at least one piece of work from every student who completed a trimester. There are plenty of analyses, ranging from close reading to broader, even intertextual discussion. There are historical, sociological, and cultural investigations, one or two of which have made startling and useful discoveries. There are parodies. There are personal responses, which I encouraged, especially at the end of the series. The quality of the work in this anthology is extraordinary, a testament to how fully and thoughtfully all of these young scholars have interacted with this work.

There is one caveat readers must keep in mind. All of these essays were written without knowledge of what would happen in *Dance's* future. When a writer suggests what events might transpire in subsequent volumes, she is doing so honestly, without actual foreknowledge of what Powell is planning. Even so, some of these predictions are extremely perceptive.

Now, a story: in December of 2005 I was in England to read a paper at the Centenary Anthony Powell Conference at the Wallace Collection. Afterwards I did some traveling around the country, stopping off in Oxford for a couple of days. Secure in my anonymity, I was walking toward Blackwell's Bookstore when a voice behind me said, "Do you still teach at Andover?"

I turned, astonished. It was Travis Pantin, whose essay "Assertions of the Will" appears in the *Buyer's Market* section. We popped off to a pub and talked for two hours; he was doing an exchange year at Jesus College. Here was a real *Dance* moment, and for anyone who feels that Powell relies too heavily on coincidence, I tell them this story. Just one more lesson my students have taught us.

One final point: all the proceeds from *Dance Class* are dedicated to the Anthony Powell Society, which has worked so hard to spread the good news about this wonderful writer. Especial thanks must be delineated for Keith Marshall, who has labored tirelessly on behalf of the society and generously in support of this book.

Note: All page references are to the University of Chicago edition of *Dance to the Music of Time*. These are equivalent to the Heinemann editions, as well as the Little, Brown ones. In the essays parenthetical unidentified page numbers always refer to the novel under discussion; the other novels will be preceded by an abbreviation, as (*BM* 15). Abbreviations are as follows:

QU – A Question of Upbringing
BM – A Buyer's Market
AW – The Acceptance World
LM – At Lady Molly's
CCR – Casanova's Chinese Restaurant
KO – The Kindly Ones
VB – The Valley of Bones
SA – The Soldier's Art
MP – The Military Philosophers

BDFR – Books Do Furnish a Room
TK – Temporary Kings
HSH – Hearing Secret Harmonies

CHAPTER 1:
A QUESTION OF UPBRINGING

The first volume of *Dance* makes a perfect place for high school seniors to begin. After all, the characters are exactly their age: in the final year of secondary school before moving on to university. They *know* these people – the Budds, the Stringhams, the Templers, and the Widmerpools. They know LaBas as well. Nick Jenkins is facing so many of their issues – self-identity, family pressures, friendship and trust, the Future – and they can agree or disagree with his decisions very easily.

The issues we had to clarify in class discussion were primarily two. First, Powell's writing style for many of the students was a shock. The long sentences with their Latinate vocabulary were a bit intimidating at first. "Good SAT prep," said one of the students. We did quite a bit of reading aloud, stopping to gloss unfamiliar words and phrases. Second, the Oxford system, with dons (what do they *do*?) was confusing. Fortunately I had a colleague, Chris Walter, who had an undergraduate degree from Oxford, and he came to one of our seminars to explain how it worked and to answer questions.

The students found no historical topics to attract them this early in the series. Instead they focused mostly on character analysis. Doug Presley and Nicole Duddy wrote trenchant analyses of Uncle Giles and J. G. Quiggin, respectively. Andy Clay was drawn to Uncle Giles as well, but for personal reasons; like Nick, he had had experience with a family trust, and wanted to compare notes. Corey Simpson wrote often of her personal affection – or dislike – for particular characters. At the start of the series she examined the narrator, Nick Jenkins, with both humor and perception.

SYNOPSIS

A Question of Upbringing begins at "School" (modeled on Eton College) in 1921. Jenkins rooms with friends Stringham and Templer, and has his first encounter with Widmerpool. Jenkins' Uncle Giles pays an unexpected visit to the house, and leaves illegal cigarette smoke in his wake. The three boys tease Le Bas, the housemaster, with the "Braddock alias Thorne" prank.

Jenkins has lunch at the Stringhams', meeting Mrs. Fox, Stringham's mother; Buster, her husband; and Tuffy Weedon, her secretary. Later, he visits the Templers' home, meeting Jean Templer, with whom he becomes infatuated; Sunny Farebrother, a fan of Templer's father; and Gwen McReith, with whom Templer is having an affair. He watches another character, Jimmy Stripling, try unsuccessfully to play a practical joke on Farebrother.

Jenkins travels to a guesthouse, La Grenadiere, in France to improve his French. Widmerpool is already at there and shows his diplomatic skill by settling an argument between two Scandinavian guests. While there Jenkins falls in love with Suzette, but when he works up the courage to express himself, he accidentally finds himself speaking to the wrong woman, Mme. Dubuisson.

At "University," or Oxford, Jenkins attends the don Sillery's teas with Stringham, where they meet other undergraduates: Mark Members, J. G. Quiggin, and recent graduate Bill Truscott. Stringham leaves Oxford and goes to work for industrialist Sir Magnus Donners with Truscott. Two significant fallouts occur - Stringham and Templer's paths diverge after a car accident; and Stringham stands up Jenkins for dinner to go on a date. Unexpectedly Jenkins dines instead with Uncle Giles.

CHARACTER LIST

The major characters in this volume, organized by chapter:

Chapter 1

Jenkins – the narrator
Uncle Giles – Jenkins' disreputable uncle
Widmerpool – an unpopular student at school
Charles Stringham – a schoolmate and friend of Jenkins
Peter Templer – a schoolmate and friend of Jenkins
Le Bas – housemaster at school

Chapter 2

Buster Foxe – Stringham's stepfather
Miss Weedon – secretary to Stringham's mother
Mrs. Foxe – Stringham's mother
Jean Templer – Templer's younger sister and Jenkins' love interest
Sunny Farebrother – an associate of Templer's father
Mr. Templer – Templer's father
Jimmy Stripling – Templer's brother-in-law, a racing motorist
Lady Gwen McReith – a Templer family friend
Babs – Templer's other sister, married to Stripling

Chapter 3

Madame and Commandant Leroy – owners of La Grenadière
Suzette – Jenkins' French love
Mme. and M. Dubuisson – guests at La Grenadière
Örn – Norwegian tennis player, guest at La Grenadière
Lundquist – Swedish tennis player, guest at La Grenadière

Chapter 4

J. G. Quiggin – scholarship student at Oxford
Mark Members – accomplished poet; student at Oxford
Sillery – don at Oxford
Bill Truscott – employee of Sir Magnus Donners
Jimmy Brent, Bob Duport – friends and business associates of Templer

Jenkins: Viewing Life Through Books
Corey Simpson

It seems rash to indicate any kind of preference so early in the series, but while reading *A Question of Upbringing*, I have grown especially attached to Jenkins, and all I can do is attempt to explain my reasons and hope he does not later turn out to be an ax-murderer. Short of his being an ax-murderer, though, I will defend him stubbornly, because, based on one quote – one casual, passing comment in the first few pages – I suspect Jenkins' entire outlook on life is colored by what I privately refer to as "bookish idealism," an affliction that has haunted me since the age of four and which gives me the greatest sympathy for his motivations.

The quote I find so revealing is actually about Templer. Jenkins is, in the beginning, not sure he likes his messmate because his "boast that he had never read a book for pleasure in his life did not predispose me in his favour: though he knew far more than I of the things about which books are written." He clearly feels strongly about books if he is inclined to dislike anyone who dislikes reading, and his lack of worldly knowledge confirms that he has probably spent more time living through his books than through the kind of experiences Peter Templer has had. Lacking such experience, Jenkins is forced to see everything he encounters as he has learned: through books.

"Bookish idealism" being an entirely invented term, I'll define it as the tendency to see life as one long, complex story, and the perpetual hope that said story will contain characters as easy to understand as those in fiction. Jenkins certainly sees his life as a story; accustomed to watching events unfold in books, he tends to do the same with his own life, narrating faithfully but rarely involving himself. He watches and analyzes others carefully, but never examines his own actions and motivations in equal depth.

Another of Jenkins's more noticeable weaknesses is his habit of leaping to absurdly detailed conclusions about people he has barely met, assigning them all sorts of qualities based on appearance or pure whim. Nowhere is this more clearly illustrated than Jenkins' preconceived picture of Sunny Farebrother – for, except in novels, people rarely fit neatly into categories, or match whatever images their names might evoke.

Most obviously idealistic of all is his attitude towards love, which is treated so casually by Templer but is extremely important to Jenkins. Jean Templer is neither exceptionally pretty nor especially polite, remaining silent for most of his visit and speaking only to make some commonplace remark – yet Jenkins attributes this to Jean's "mysterious, even melancholy, presence." This is far less believable than Stringham's melancholy; it would be acceptable if he had actually known Jean, but Jenkins wastes no time in comparing her to a sad young saint, a tragic martyr to tennis.

Later, in France, his encounter with Suzette makes him aware of "that restless sense of something desired that had become an increasing burden upon both day and night." He wants to love someone, even needs to be in love; so why not assign his desired qualities to girls too aloof to disturb his carefully crafted ideal? It is probably no coincidence that, straight from several years of living with and admiring Stringham, Jenkins is inclined to label anyone he wants to like as "melancholy." Upon arriving in France, he falls for Suzette easily, instantly "seeing" in her the same emotional intensity he believes he has seen in Jean, although at that point he knows nothing about Suzette except her liking for writing letters in mauve ink.

Jenkins' belief that first impressions and speculation can provide an accurate picture of any person is one that could only be practical in fiction; the constant evolution of his acquaintances show that real life doesn't work that way. He possesses an odd combination of accurate observation and wild imagination; though he has all the qualities of a good narrator, he can't be regarded as reliable until he can bring the two into balance.

UNCLE GILES: THROUGH THE HAZE
DOUGLAS PRESLEY

Despite Uncle Giles' repeated disappearances throughout the first book, he nevertheless permeates the story. He is regarded by Jenkins as an eccentric abnormality in life, someone out of touch with the world, and clueless as to how society works. Yet, upon closer analysis, Giles seems truly to have a deeper understanding of how the world operates, and the more that Jenkins thinks about his uncle, the more respect he seems to gain for him. By first portraying Giles as an extreme end of the human spectrum, then slowly revealing that he is not so odd after all, Powell demonstrates that opportunities to learn can come from even the strangest of sources.

Upon first meeting this interesting character, we are presented with the image of a sad, irresponsible figure. "Even those who [had] known him for years sometimes found difficulty in estimating the lengths to which he could carry his lack of reliability" (65) proclaims Jenkins, still unsure of how to properly classify his uncle. He elaborates "Uncle Giles had been relegated by most of the people who knew him at all well to that limbo where nothing is expected of a person" (16). Both of these comments, along with the many other disparaging remarks made by Jenkins, serve to establish the extent to which Giles does not fit into society, in the eyes of the narrator. He is irresponsible; he shows up uninvited, and then disappears without any contact, as if he never existed. Our first encounters with Giles set him apart as someone completely out of touch with society. The argument that Uncle Giles hardly exists is not hard to make: later in the book, Stringham has no recollection of him, even though his visit is portrayed as a major incident in the mind of Jenkins. Giles's prolonged disappearances serve as a haze, blocking him from view.

We are also presented with the fact that Jenkins does not know his uncle all that well. There had been a "severance of relations"

(22) between his father and uncle, and Jenkins questions whether his uncle has "quite a lot of fun" or if he "lives in perpetual hell" (25), demonstrating a void of information about him. As Jenkins grows older, wiser, and is exposed to Giles more frequently, his uncle seems more and more normal. During the tea at Sillery's, Jenkins ventures so far as to state that "Uncle Giles's untiring contortions before the altar of the Trust, when considered in this light, now began to appear less grotesque than formerly" (172-3). We also know that Jenkins does not understand his uncle clearly yet, for as he says himself "[he] did not in those days see [Giles] with anything like this clearness of vision" (17). At the time Jenkins does not know his uncle well enough to pass judgment on him fairly.

While Jenkins fails firmly to establish his uncle as "unreliable," Giles manages to portray himself, now and then, as quite astute. Though he seems to act outside of the spectrum of normal behavior, he nevertheless believes that "rules are made to be obeyed." (19). If in practice he is abnormal, at least he is able to think clearly. Uncle Giles certainly has a few odd tendencies, yet overall, he seems like he is in complete control of himself, for as Jenkins states "it [had] to be admitted that [he was] unusually well equipped for looking after himself" (23).

Jenkins leaves us with a few lingering thoughts about Giles at the close of the first book. Jenkins sets up the expectation that he will grow fonder of Giles in the coming texts, especially when he states that he "dismissed Uncle Giles letter from [his] mind, as [he] now thinks, rather inexcusably" (220-1). We leave the chapter with a final image of Giles, in contrast to our original idea of him, reading *Some Things That Matter*, quite a contrast from someone who "took not the slightest interest in anyone or anything except himself" (19-20). While Giles is unquestionably strange, he gets progressively more normal as the plot advances. The development of his character through the story reveals a depth that Jenkins is only slowly coming to discover. Jenkins is starting to learn that knowledge can be acquired even from the most unexpected sources, and that no one is truly insignificant.

After all, in the words of Le Bas, "it takes all sorts to make a world" (224).

QUESTIONING QUIGGIN: HIS MANNERISMS AND MOTIVES
NICOLE DUDDY

From his unkempt appearance to his coarse and frank manner of conversation, J.G. Quiggin presents himself as an unappealing yet peculiar personality, capable of making an impression on everyone he encounters. First acquaintances are usually hesitant in the sense that they never want to give bad first impressions or to strike others as unlikable human beings. However, when he bursts into the room, rudely banging open the door in an unapologetic manner and taking a seat with a sour look on his face, Quiggin makes it apparent that he does not practice this common exercise of caution among an unfamiliar audience. Jenkins can already tell that Quiggin is special; he comments "For the first time since coming up I felt that I was at last getting into touch with the submerged element of the university, which, I had sometimes suspected, might have more to offer than was to be found in conventional undergraduate circles" (179). Indeed, Quiggin defies the conventionality among the standard undergraduates at the university, and perhaps what makes him different fuels his ambitions to rise up from his modest background.

Quiggin is, no doubt, a very opinionated individual and an aggressive inquisitor. When Sillery asks him the simple question "Are you happy?" he begins to "enlarge on the matter of his own exasperation. He said: 'All anyone here seems interested in is in messing about... I thought people came to the university to study, not to booze and gas all the time.'"(181).

After that, everyone seems a little taken aback by such an attack on the university. In response, Sillery says, "You find we all fall woefully short of your own exacting standards – formed, no doubt, in a more austere tradition." (181). While they walk together, Quiggin persistently questions Jenkins "without relaxing [his] harsh exterior" (201), as if probing for valuable information. He also claims to hate anything superficial; he would much rather read *Fabian Essays in Socialism* compared to the popular novel, *The Green Hat*, which describes the life of the rich and lost generation. He adds: "I suppose that depicts the kind of world that your friend Stringham will enter..." (203). Jenkins also discovers that Quiggin is keen on meeting people he considers important, as if it was an opportunity to judge their worth or build his own connections.

What are the roots to such an attitude of self-assurance? Quiggin's grating voice, with its Northern Country inflexion, reveals his modest background, though talk of his hometown is something he wants to avoid. Quiggin makes it well known that he is not rich like his contemporaries, perhaps even exaggerating a bit. His lack of money translates into a deficiency in class, status, a first-rate primary education, a distinguished family name, etc. On the subject of Bill Truscott and the job opportunity as private secretary to Sir Magnus Donners, Quiggin says, "I knew at once there would be no chance of Truscott thinking of me. Not good enough, I suppose... Not good enough by a long chalk" (204). His envy and discontent, for Stringham in this case, encourages him to surpass the superficial privileged upper class – the Stringhams who get the jobs because of their connections. This requires a lot of self-discipline on his part. He has done so already by "collect[ing] unto himself sundry scholarships and exhibitions, which ... is much to his credit" (177).

Ultimately, Quiggin will stay a topic of interest among the circle of undergraduates on matters of his background, appearance, and "something of the angry solitude of spirit that [holds Jenkins'] attention..." (205). Above all, Jenkins must not sympathize with Quiggin, who shows the will, independence, and capacity to take care of himself. As Sillery assures Jenkins, "Quiggin is an able young man... we must not forget that" (212). His display of work ethic and ambition might take him places farther than anyone would like to imagine.

©Nicole Duddy, 2007

TRUSTS: THE JENKINS AND CLAY FAMILY TRUSTS
ANDY CLAY

Family trusts and other forms of inherited wealth can breed weird and embarrassing behavior among family members. The purpose of a family trust is to pass the earned wealth of one generation on to the next. However, when divided among multiple individuals, trusts can bring turmoil to a family. In the opening chapter of *A Question of Upbringing*, the narrator, Jenkins, introduces his Uncle Giles as an abnormal, unreliable character obsessed with the Jenkins family trust. According to Jenkins, "nothing [Uncle Giles] does can ever be accepted as serious" (16). Uncle Giles's obsession with the trust is revealed by his unannounced arrival in Jenkins's dorm at Eton. Similarly, my grandparents were also obsessed with the terms of the two family trusts of which they were members. Like Uncle Giles, my grandparents too were awkward to be around.

The trust money that my grandparents received came from two family trusts – one set up by my grandfather's family and the other by my grandmother's. John Clay, my grandfather's grandfather, was a successful businessman and rancher in Wyoming. After his death, his grandchildren placed what was remaining of his estate and fortune in a trust, in order to protect the money from John Clay Jr., who was a big spender. On my grandmother's side there was another trust. The Rogers family, a successful landowning family in Chicago during the early 20th century, put the family fortune into a trust, of which my grandmother and her two siblings were members.

For both Uncle Giles and my grandparents, the trust money did not solve any financial problems. When describing the trust, Jenkins says, "Uncle Giles has never been satisfied that he was receiving the full amount to which he was by right entitled: so that when times were hard – which happened about every eighteen months – he used to apply pressure with a view to squeezing out a few pounds more than his agreed position" (22). Whereas

Jenkins's father has made his own living, Uncle Giles is incapable of living within his means and instead relies on the money from the trust routinely to fallback on. Additionally, Uncle Giles's obsession about the trust damages his relationship with both Jenkins and Jenkins's father, Uncle Giles's brother. Uncle Giles's routine attempts to change the terms of the trust, as Jenkins describes, "had the effect of making my father exceedingly angry; and ... they had resulted in an almost complete severance of relations between the two brothers" (22) As a result, the family trust ironically tears apart the Jenkins family.

Likewise, the trust money inherited by my grandparents disrupted my family more than it helped. Before they even received the money from the two trusts, my grandparents borrowed against it to go on exotic vacations and live a life of luxury. On a side note, my grandparents did not once consider spending money on their children. "Granny," my dad's grandmother, paid for his Andover and MIT education. In the long run, this created a rift between my father and his parents. After paying of their debts following the dispersion of the trust money in the early '90s, my grandparents had little-to-no money to spend or borrow against. However, just as Uncle Giles fails to live within his means, my grandparents were not able to be self-sufficient and relied on the financial support of their children, including my dad, to fall back on. In the same way Uncle Giles and his brother drift apart because of the trust, the relationship between my father and his parents broke apart as a result of money issues.

The behavior of both Uncle Giles and my grandparents, though different, makes it embarrassing to be around them. Uncle Giles's unexpected appearance at Eton creates an awkward situation between him, Jenkins, and Stringham. Jenkins describes his uncle's entrance by saying, "At first ... he did not venture to advance farther into the room, meekly conscious that his unexpected arrival might ... be regarded by the occupants as creating a pivot for potential embarrassment" (p.15). In fact, the real purpose of Uncle's Giles's visit, embarrassingly, is to find the whereabouts of Jenkins's father, in order to ask for a bigger share of the trust.

In a similar way, my grandparents, especially my grandfather, acted arrogantly, and, like Uncle Giles, were embarrassing to be around. On several occasions, my grandfather would boast about the exotic vacations and first class flights he had taken. Yet he failed to state that he was spending money that he himself did not earn. After my grandparents spent most of the trust money, though, they became increasingly like Uncle Giles, routinely asking for money to pay their bills.

While family trusts are nice free sources of income, they tend to breed strange, embarrassing behavior in family members. In addition, trusts and inherited wealth allow people, like Uncle Giles and my grandparents, to live off the work of others rather than their own merit or entrepreneurship.

CHAPTER 2:
A BUYER'S MARKET

The students, not surprisingly, understood at once that the primary commodity in *A Buyer's Market* is love. It's a party book, after all; Nick Jenkins goes from one to another of them – six in all: the Walpole-Wilsons' dinner, the Huntercombes' ball, Milly Andriadis's louche affair in the Duports' house, the Walpole-Wilsons' house party, Sir Magnus's luncheon, and dinner with the Widmerpools. Love and Lust fill all the air of the novel, and parties are where young people go to breathe such breezes.

Not surprisingly, then, almost every paper at least mentioned love or sex, and one-half (12 of 24) were explicitly focused on the love lives of one or more characters. Luke Spears discusses the two forms of love Nick Jenkins experiences, emotional (with Barbara Goring) and "venal" (with Gypsy Jones). Travis Pantin considers the role of "will" in pursuing amorous matters; he is the first person in either class to begin to notice this theme – of power and will – that becomes so significant throughout *Dance*. Jimmy Yang is the first to examine the significance of Jean Templer; her importance is so subtly foreshadowed in the first two books (at least until the last paragraph of *A Buyer's Market*) that none of the other students remarked on her as a market commodity Nick might seriously imagine himself possessing. Finally, Matt Cranney creates the first parody of the course – Gypsy Jones musing about her affair with Nick. It is a remarkably sophisticated piece, with lots of insight into that rather grubby nymph.

A Buyer's Market begins with a flashback to Paris just after the War when the Jenkinses meet Mr. Deacon in the Louvre. The narrative jumps to London in 1928 at the Walpole-Wilsons', where Jenkins is attending a dinner party with his love interest, Barbara Goring. After dinner they go to the Huntercombes' dance, where Barbara, in a joke gone awry, pours sugar over Widmerpool's head. Jenkins and Widmerpool leave the dance soon afterwards, and meet Deacon and Gypsy Jones in the street. They encounter Stringham, who invites them all to another party.

Stringham brings Jenkins, Mr. Deacon, Gypsy Jones, and Widmerpool to Milly Andriadis's party. The bohemian atmosphere of the party sharply contrasts with that of the Huntercombes. Jenkins sees Sillery and Prince Theodoric and admires Baby Wentworth and Bijou Ardglass. Widmerpool drinks too much and admires Gypsy. Mr. Deacon fights with Max Pilgrim about his risqué song, and Stringham quarrels with Milly and leaves. At the end of the evening, Uncle Giles' appears outside Nick's flat.

Jenkins speaks with Barnby about Baby Wentworth; then he visits the Walpole-Wilsons in the country for a "house party." The party is asked to lunch at Stourwater, Sir Magnus Donners's castle. Here they meet Prince Theodoric and with Truscott and Stringham tour the dungeon - where, says Sir Magnus, "we should put the girls who don't behave." Jenkins meets up with Jean Templer – who is now married to Bob Duport – and also with Widmerpool, who is still upset at having to pay for Gypsy's abortion, and who later backs his car into a huge stone urn in the castle keep.

At his birthday party Deacon has an accident and dies. Jenkins attends his funeral, meeting Quiggin and Members there. Later, Jenkins returns to Deacon's shop, where he finds Gypsy, dressed as Eve, and loses his virginity to her. He then goes to the Widmerpools' for dinner where Janice Walpole-Wilson reveals Barbara's engagement to Pardoe.

—————————— CHARACTER LIST ——————————

The major characters in this volume, organized by chapter:

Chapter 1

Mr. Deacon – eccentric artist, friend of Jenkins's parents
Barbara Goring – crush of Jenkins, niece of Lady Walpole-Wilson
Sir Gavin Walpole-Wilson – former diplomat
Lady Walpole-Wilson – wife of Sir Gavin
Eleanor Walpole-Wilson – troublesome daughter of Walpole-Wilsons
Archie Gilbert – handsome, well-dressed, frequent partygoer
Johnny Pardoe – ladies' man, wealthy
Tomsitt – another suitor for Barbara
Gypsy Jones – friend of Mr. Deacon's, rather sluttish but attractive

Chapter 2

Milly Andriadis – hostess of the party, also Stringham's mistress
Max Pilgrim – gay pianist at the party
Sillery – an Oxford don
Prince Theodoric – Balkan royalty
Bijou Ardglass – an aristocratic and good-looking blonde
Baby Wentworth – Sir Magnus Donners' lover
Sir Magnus Donners – the "Chief," Stringham and Truscott's boss
Uncle Giles – Jenkins' uncle

Chapter 3

Barnby – a painter living above Deacon's shop

Chapter 4

Quiggin and Members – Jenkins' acquaintances from Oxford
Mrs. Widmerpool – Widmerpool's mother
Miss Walpole Wilson – Eleanor's aunt

* * *

Haiku

Banana in eyes,
Widmerpool's face is slavish:
Now it's Barbara's turn.
                    - Gauri Kirloskar

An Intricate Business: Early Love in Dance
Luke Spears

In the first two books of *A Dance to the Music of Time*, we see a narrator struggling with the concept of love. Nick's initially reserved and reflective approach to relationships amounts to little in *A Question of Upbringing*, and is perhaps overshadowed by the increasing number of "conquests" made by Stringham and Templer (106). In *A Buyer's Market*, Nick takes a step beyond the almost completely one-sided love affairs he has had with Jean Templer and Suzette, and into a relationship with the vivacious Barbara Goring. With Barbara, Nick comes closer to experiencing mutual love, and though this is fulfilling for a time, its shortcomings eventually give rise to an emotional conflict within him. Ultimately, he finds flaws in Barbara, including her disapproval of "sentimentality" and her occasional (habitual?) carelessness, and he ends the affair (23). Not soon after this, driven perhaps by a desire to balance out his previous experience with love, or by a sense of falling behind his contemporaries, Nick engages in a rather awkward one-night stand with the "sluttish" Gypsy Jones. Thus, by the end of *A Buyer's Market*, he has had a fuller, if somewhat less usual, experience with the world of love, and seems prepared to venture further into it with greater success.

In *A Question of Upbringing*, Nick's attitude toward love, sex, and relationships, perhaps because it is addressed only in limited terms, seems hesitant. He is timid about voicing his feelings for both Jean and Suzette, and this results not only in no real relationship developing with either girl, but also in a feeling of regret. He is hurt when Jean doesn't pay him much attention and associates with other men at the Horabins' dance, but he also realizes that he has never had any "prescriptive rights" to her, and that she hasn't had any way of knowing how he felt (94). With Suzette, Nick at least attempts to make known his feelings – he holds her hand at one point, and later attempts to verbally express his love to her. Unfortunately, he not only waits until his last day at La Grenadière to do the latter, but also ends up conveying his feelings to the wrong woman!

In contrast with Nick's immature love life in *A Question of Upbringing* is that of Templer, who is easy-going and successful in the game of love, as demonstrated by his fling with a "tart" while at Eton, and his affair with Lady McReith. It is difficult to say whether or not Nick approves of Templer's approach, but he does comment on it: "anyone who is prepared to pretend that love is a simple, straightforward business is always in a strong position for making conquests" (106). It is clear that Nick is not prepared to pretend this, and by the end of *A Question of Upbringing*, we have little sense of what he is prepared to do with regard to love.

At the start of *A Buyer's Market*, however, we see that Nick has developed with Barbara Goring a relationship more mature than those with Jean and Suzette. Because it is his closest experience with reciprocal love, he views the relationship initially with optimism and enthusiasm. Possibly he does not bother describing the best moments of his relationship with Barbara, but from what we see in Chapter One, there are several distinctly negative aspects to it. For one thing, Barbara does not seem committed, or even especially interested in Nick. When inviting him to dinner at the Walpole-Wilsons' she gives the impression that Nick was not the first person she has asked, and at the dinner and subsequent dance she pays him barely any notice (25). In addition, she "crook[s] her finger" at Tompsitt when he enters the room, and is involved – we can only guess how intimately – with Widmerpool (42). Barbara also possesses several personal characteristics that appear to irritate Nick, including egotism, capriciousness, and an excessive exuberance. These qualities prompt Nick to wonder if he "so far from loving [Barbara], [does] not actually hate her," and ultimately they play a part in his decision, made after she pours sugar over Widmerpool's head, that she is not and never was right for him (73).

Nick also learns a lesson about the difference between "emotional" and "venal" attraction in *A Buyer's Market*. Barbara's aversion to "sentimentality" – and the general lack of any physical side to the relationship between Barbara and Nick – beside probably playing a role in Nick's decision to no longer pursue her, also gives Nick a somewhat one-sided experience with love, as was the case with his earlier adventures. Nick's exclusion from the world of sexual love with Barbara, coupled with the fact that Stringham, Templer, and even Widmerpool seem to have outpaced him with respect to the number and maturity of their love affairs, drives him to "not lightly pass by" the opportunity to sleep with Gypsy Jones (256). Nick himself remarks on the similarities between Gypsy and Barbara: they seem to share both a slightly annoying exuberance and a certain egotism (258). It seems to me that the two girls each embody a different side of love; Barbara represents emotional love, and Gypsy sexual, or "venal" love.

Combining his experiences with Barbara and Gypsy, Nick completes his introduction into the world of love. However, while he may have once professed to be "in love" with Barbara, and did commit the physical act of love with Gypsy, whether he truly loves either of them is questionable. His comment that Barbara "was not – and had never been – for [him]," plus his feelings of "alienation," "inadequacy," and even "shock" directly after lying with Gypsy, suggest that Nick, at least as he looks back, feels no great fondness for either woman. Overall, though his initiation into the world of love is not altogether positive, he has crossed a meaningful threshold, and is ready to attempt further "conquests" by merging his experiences with Barbara and his experiences with Gypsy.

Assertions of the Will
Travis Pantin

During the first and second books of Anthony Powell's series *A Dance to the Music of Time*, the contrasting emotional and professional lives of Nick Jenkins, the narrator, and Kenneth Widmerpool, the sometime antagonist/sometime protagonist, reveal one of their deep-rooted differences. The emotional and professional schism forming between Jenkins and Widmerpool originates from a fundamental contrast in their usage of the will. During these books, Widmerpool seems to be acting in accordance with some sort of premeditated design, while Jenkins, the observer, usually steps back from his immediate surroundings letting the eddies and flows of *Dance* carry him where they will.

Throughout the first two books, the pursuit of the opposite sex seems to be a race, one in which Jenkins has fallen far behind his friends. These friends, Stringham and Templer, provide a reference frame for the reader to clearly see Jenkins' inability to progress emotionally or physically with women. Jenkins, trailing further and further behind, accepts his estrangement from most of society by admitting even "Widmerpool capable of possessing a vigorous emotional life of his own" (169). At this point, Widmerpool – who had earlier been portrayed as barely human – enters the race with relative success. Suddenly, Jenkins finds himself contending with Widmerpool for women, and soon notices that if either of them has the upper hand, it is Widmerpool.

At the Walpole-Wilson's party, after witnessing Widmerpool's "vigorous and instantaneous assertion of the will" towards Barbara Goring, Nick feels an "emancipation from regarding Barbara as [his] own especial concern" (69). This instance applies to almost all of Widmerpool and Jenkins' relationships with women. Widmerpool usually takes deliberate action towards a defined end, while Jenkins feels his emotions have "taken place" (or not)(112), and he follows them not deliberately, but "somnambulistic[ally]," only when he encounters a "lack of demur"(256).

In comparison to Widmerpool, Jenkins also has little professional motivation so far. Throughout the book, Widmerpool tries to give pep talks to Jenkins about the importance of one's work and professional standing. Their contrasting views appear clearly when Widmerpool says he "can't see [Jenkins' job] leading to much," and Jenkins replies, "What ought it to lead to?" (79)

However, Jenkins soon becomes bitter towards people like Quiggin and Widmerpool, those "who have decided to live by the force of the will" (239). By admitting to himself that "this matter of making headway in life was one to which I felt I ... ought to devote greater consideration in future," (133) he not only demonstrates envy for the benefits Widmerpool is beginning to reap, but shows a conscious ideological separation from him.

By the end of the second book, we find Jenkins, a bachelor of relatively weak professional standing, alone and estranged from many of his childhood acquaintances. Perhaps, Jenkins' sudden affinity towards Mr. Deacon's social circle results from a discomfort in the awareness that his older friends, many now married and well employed, are beginning to alienate him. At the closing of *A Buyer's Market*, Jenkins stands to be irreparably separated from many of those with whom he grew up if he does not soon manage to muster some sort of emotional or professional momentum.

©Travis Pantin, 2001

Jean Templer: A Very Different Love Interest
Jimmy Yang

When Nick Jenkins first meets Jean Templer on a visit to the Templer home, in the first volume of *A Dance to the Music of Time*, he is captivated by her strange, almost otherworldly appearance. She is a mystery to him, saying only two sentences, about how "the hard court needs resurfacing" and informing Peter that Sunny Farebrother "turned up just after he left," (*QU*, 74) She seems to pay no heed at all to Nick. He believes himself in love with her, however, despite the apparent lack of interest on her part; and the fact that she is only "fair, not strikingly pretty" does not deter him. (74)

In the second book, *A Buyer's Market*, we meet Jean again, and she still remains an enigma to Nick. The two have not met since his prior visit, and she only appears for a fleeting second in this book. That second, however, gives us insight into his feelings for her, and, in a brief note at the end of the book, how their relationship may develop in the future. Whether she will remain a love interest to him remains to be seen, but what is certain is that their relationship will grow, and it will take quite unexpected turns.

The female characters in the foreground of *A Buyer's Market* are for the most part, unmarried. As such, Jean, who is now married to Bob Duport, seems as though she would be thrust into the background. In fact, she does enter the story for only a moment, but in that moment she has a great effect on Nick. She enters just as many of Powell's characters do: without warning, and diving straight into conversation. At first, Nick does not even notice her when they are at the party at Stourwater, and she catches him "deep in the tapestry" (192). After beginning a conversation on the topic of the sin it depicts – Lust – the two catch up, just as old friends might, about times past. It is clear, however, that Jean is oblivious to Nick's old feelings. She is even so bold at the end of their meeting as to invite Nick over to visit herself and her husband, whom we know he loathes.

One angle from which we can approach Jean's character is by looking at Barbara Goring, who is Nick's love interest at the beginning of *A Buyer's Market*. Barbara is flirtatious, and, as Nick finds out near the beginning, leads several men on – Widmerpool, Tompsitt, and Nick himself. She does not commit to any one of the men who are after her, telling Nick, "don't get sentimental" (23), and acting in a similarly flighty manner with the other men. She also seems very shallow. This can be seen in the conversation about the Haig Statue, appearing almost comical in her out-of-place statement, "I can't see why they can't make a model of a real horse. Couldn't they do it in plaster of Paris or something. Don't you think?'" (40) All of this together slowly worsens Nick's impression of her. The last event that pushes him over the edge, however, is her pouring sugar all over Widmerpool. While Nick begins *A Buyer's Market* positively enamored by her, by the end of the first chapter he is disillusioned, and has decided that he will stop seeing her.

Jean is very different from Barbara Goring. She has a much more serious air. She is not beautiful, but she seems to be a much more mature person, with "a sense of restraint, a reserve at present unpredictable" (191). In Nick's own words, she "seemed to express none of the qualities I had liked in Barbara" (191). Nick finds this much more agreeable, as, at this point, he is attempting to do as much as possible to remove himself from Barbara.

Nick and Jean, however, are not likely to have any sort of romantic relationship any time in the near future. He expresses himself that, as a married woman, Jean in his mind is "removed automatically from any such sphere of interest" (214). She most certainly does not share Nick's dislike for Bob Duport, since she married him, and, by the end of *A Buyer's Market*, we find out that she is "expecting" (234). One glimmer of hope for Nick, however, tells us that we will see more of Jean in the future; that their relationship may yet change again (as so many things have done so far in Powell's story), and that these two characters will grow closer together. "Certain stages of experience might be compared to a game of Russian billiards, played (as I used to play with Jean, when the time came) on those small green tables..." (274) We do not know how their relationship will develop, only that it will grow, and it will be quite unlike Nick's relationships with other women.

©James Yang, 2007

All In a Day's Work: The Deflowering of Nick Jenkins
Matthew Cranney

Today was one of those peculiar days, one of those days that represent a transition into another phase of life. I can't believe that Edgar is dead. I'll be frank, I'm going to miss the old man. I chose not to go to the funeral. Organized religion is such a disservice to the dead. Instead, I went out for a drink. He would find this a more suitable celebration of his life, and I feel that if I don't stand by my principles then I'm no sort of person at all. It is unfortunate that horrid woman, his sister, couldn't see eye to eye with me.

I had a little run in with that fellow Jenkins this afternoon, the stuck-up one who's always coming over to chat with Barnby. He surprised me a little. I was trying on my Eve costume for the Fancy Dress party, and I was going to show it to Barnby. The dress is just the sort that he'd abhor, but I think it's a fetching little number. And apparently Mr. Jenkins agrees. I was happy to see he has a little libido left in him. He simply proves my philosophy that everyone needs a good f#ck every once in a bit. I do think it may have been his first time. It was a rather awkward little debacle. Still, I relish that sensation of losing Self and melding into one. It is more potent than the finest opium. I do hope it did him some good, but I don't know if it helped him loosen up. He was quick to make an exit after we were done. I even tried to be friendly. I enquired into the details of the funeral, not that they made the faintest difference. He did mention something about Max Pilgrim, which gave me a good laugh after he left. I admire the pansy garden's sense of community: it seems to conquer the most bitter of personal rivalries. I can't say I wasn't glad to see Jenkins go. Howard came over shortly after. Howard is a forward-thinking fellow, but men get jealous so easy, and I still need a place to stay.

All of these men, constantly thinking they are so fantastic simply because they're on top. Ugh, perhaps it is time for me to take another venture to the Island of Lesbos (as Edgar so elegantly put it). The softness of a woman provides a nice contrast. I don't understand why our modern society is so set on its sexual boundaries. The Greeks were more sophisticated than we are, and that was millennia ago! Now they view homosexuality or any aberration from their social norm as madness and immorality. But they view nothing wrong in mowing down millions of young men with their machine guns. And for no good reason! At least with a f#ck you get some pleasure out of it. This world can be a cruel place, so why is everyone so hell bent on deciding how people get their kicks. I know I'm only trying to cope as best I can.

CHAPTER 3:
THE ACCEPTANCE WORLD

The third volume of *Dance* is the last that has built-in, personal, high school appeal. It still focuses pretty heavily on erotic love; after all, Nick and Jean conduct a reasonably torrid affair, and that kind of behavior always sells at the box office of adolescence. When Jean opens the door wearing "nothing but a pair of slippers," well, the students know that Nick has left that twitty little Barbara Goring in the dust.

But there's another theme in *The Acceptance World* that is every bit as important to seniors in high school as love, and that is career. As Ash Verdery points out in his perceptive essay, the "acceptance world" as defined by Templer refers both to romance and to commerce. Jenkins and the others are making decisions about the sort of work they will devote their lives to.

One of the real gifts of teaching *Dance* is that it is genuinely interdisciplinary: students can profitably write papers that fit into any number of disciplines. Jason Myung, who was taking an economics course at the same time he was reading Powell, took up the challenge of making sense out of Widmerpool's Old Boy address. As one who has never studied economics, I have had, as they say, to rely on the kindness of strangers; a colleague in the History and Social Science Department at Andover, Carroll Perry, was good enough to help me evaluate Jason's effort – which made good sense to him. Widmerpool *is*, in fact, saying something.

Cassidy Carpenter made a completely original discovery in her essay, which explains Mrs. Erdleigh's fortune-telling methods. She has found out the date of Nicholas Jenkins's birthday – and it is a significant day indeed. By the way, Cassidy's essay is the first in this collection (but not the last) that uses outside sources. I should say that, because the primary demands of the course were taken up in reading, I gave the students lots of latitude in researching, which is to say, I allowed them to use the Internet freely. For some readers there will be far too many references to

Wikipedia and other less-than-scholarly sources. All I can say is that I have full confidence that the points the students are documenting are fully supportable.

The final essay I've selected shows a remarkable degree of maturity. I had sensed, but never really articulated, Powell's tolerance, even affection, for his homosexual characters – Mr. Deacon, Max Pilgrim, Eleanor Walpole-Wilson, Norah Tolland, *et al.* I was delighted that Mike Donelan chose to develop a discussion of that subject, even using it to define contrasting responses to Nick and Peter Templer. All in all, it was clear to me that my students found much of the familiar in the first three books of *Dance*, despite the generational and cultural divide between them and the Dancers.

Synopsis

The Acceptance World begins in London in 1931. Jenkins meets Uncle Giles for tea at the Ufford Hotel, where he is introduced to Mrs. Erdleigh. She "lays out the cards" for him, predicting a relationship with a woman in his future. Jenkins later discusses with Barnby his trouble getting the author St. John Clarke to write an introduction for his firm's book on the painter Isbister.

Jenkins goes to the Ritz to meet with Mark Members, the secretary of the author St. John Clarke, to discuss Clarke's writing an introduction to a book on the art of Horace Isbister. There he runs into Peter Templer and agrees to eat with him, his wife Mona, and Jean Templer Duport (now separated from her husband, Bob). J.G. Quiggin arrives late in place of Members as Clarke's new secretary, and they talk briefly about a piece by Clarke for a book Jenkins is publishing. Quiggin leaves and, after dinner, Jenkins agrees to stay with the Templers for the night, and on the drive to the Templers' home he begins a love affair with Jean.

Mona asks Jenkins to invite Quiggin over to join them for lunch, along with Templer, Jean, and guests Jimmy Stripling and Mrs. Erdleigh. They decide to play Planchette, a fortune-telling game, against the advice of Mrs. Erdleigh. Planchette writes to Quiggin with words from Karl Marx and suggests that St. John Clarke is sick. Quiggin leaves and Jean agrees to have Jenkins over to her flat on Friday.

Jenkins attends an exhibition of the late Isbister's paintings, where he meets Quiggin. Afterwards, with Mark Members he witnesses a hunger march, in which Sillery, Quiggin, Mona, and St. John Clarke participate. He goes to Jean's, where he learns of her former affair with Jimmy Stripling. They go to Foppa's, where he meets Barnby and Anne Stepney, and later Dicky Umfraville. Guggenbühl shows up with Mrs. Andriadis before Jenkins and Jean leave together.

Jenkins attends one of Le Bas' Old Boy Dinners, where Templer tells him that Mona has left him for Quiggin. A week or two earlier Jenkins learned that Quiggin had been replaced by Guggenbühl as St. John Clarke's secretary. Stringham shows up at the dinner, intoxicated. Then Widmerpool makes an unwelcome speech about economics. Le Bas has a stroke. Jenkins takes Stringham (now extremely intoxicated) home. Widmerpool appears and helps Jenkins deal with Stringham. Jenkins goes to Jean's flat and learns that her husband is returning to London.

CHARACTER LIST

The major characters in this volume, organized by chapter:

Chapter 1

Nick Jenkins – narrator
Uncle Giles – Jenkins's uncle
Mrs. Erdleigh – fortune teller; predicts Jenkins' future
Barnby – a painter, a friend of Jenkins

Chapter 2

Peter Templer – school classmate of Jenkins', businessman
Mona – former model and current wife of Peter Templer
J.G. Quiggin – university friend of Jenkins', St John Clarke's secretary
Jean Duport – Templer's sister, estranged wife of Bob Duport

Chapter 3

Jimmy Stripling – Templer's ex-brother-in-law, now involved with Mrs. Erdleigh

Chapter 4

St. John Clarke – a novelist
Mark Members – St. John Clarke's former secretary, at university with Jenkins and Quiggin
Sillery – Jenkins's former don at university
Anne Stepney – ex-sister-in-law of Stringham
Dicky Umfraville – slim, "horsy," knew Stringham in Kenya
Milly Andriadis – hostess of parties, once infatuated with Stringham
Guggenbühl – a Trotskyite, involved with Mrs. Andriadis

Chapter 5

LaBas – Jenkins's housemaster at "School"
Tolland – older "old boy" at the dinner
Brandreth – "old boy," a doctor
Maiden, Fettiplace-Jones – "old boys"
Widmerpool – special "old boy"

Prediction and Acceptance in The Acceptance World
Ash Verdery

Anthony Powell's *The Acceptance World* is not about the "acceptance world" as Templer describes it. Instead, it narrates Nick's acceptance into a significant world, the world of love, as well as many other worlds, such as the world of art. Accurate prediction forms a major theme of the novel; Nick's acceptance into the world of love – acceptance by his first real love, Jean – is predicted in two ways: through Mrs. Erdleigh's intentional divination when she reads his tarot, and through Templer's metaphor when he describes the "acceptance world" for Nick:

> If you have goods you want to sell to a firm in Bolivia, you probably do not touch your money in the ordinary way until the stuff arrives there. Certain houses, therefore, are prepared to 'accept' the debt. They will advance you the money on the strength of your reputation. It is all right when the going is good, but sooner or later you are tempted to plunge. Then there is an alteration in the value of the Bolivian exchange, or a revolution, or perhaps the firm just goes bust – and you find yourself stung. That is, if you guess wrong. (45)

Though he intends to describe only the economic world, Templer's portrayal relates two types of acceptance worlds: literally the financial world; and symbolically the world of love, represented by Nick's relationship with Jean. This description links these two worlds and contributes to the theme of accurate prediction, because his precise description of the first world also acts as a symbolic description of the second. The theme of accurate prediction is conveyed in two ways throughout the novel: through the fulfillment of an intentional divination – Mrs. Erdleigh's – and through the fulfillment of a metonymic description – Templer's.

Mrs. Erdleigh reads the cards for Nick during their first encounter:

> I expect he wants to hear about love.... This is a much more important lady – medium hair, I should say – and I think you have run across her once or twice before, though not recently. But there seems to be another man interested, too. He might even be a husband. You don't like him much. He is tallish, I should guess. Fair, possibly red hair. In business. Often goes abroad. (15)

This divination from the cards exemplifies the theme of accurate description in the novel. The "important lady" of whom she speaks is Jean, whose redheaded husband, Bob Duport, Nick despises, as he relates in chapter three of *A Question of Upbringing*. Nick's relationship with Jean demonstrates the truth of Mrs. Erdleigh's reading, which demonstrates the intentional divination aspect of the major theme.

Templer's definition of the "acceptance world" both describes the world that Duport and Widmerpool are entering and outlines the progression of Nick's relationship with Jean. Nick "has goods that he wants to sell to a firm in Bolivia," which she symbolizes, but does not touch his currency "in the ordinary way until the stuff arrives there." He gives his love, the goods, to her but does not collect the profit of this until it arrives, until she first recognizes his feelings in the cab, when: "I took Jean in my arms" (65). Templer's description continues to outline their relationship: "then there is an alteration in the value of the Bolivian exchange, or a revolution, or perhaps the firm just goes bust-and you find yourself stung." The alteration that occurs in their relationship is the imminent return of Duport, which represents a possible revolution in the love affair. Though never directly stated, Nick and Jean's relationship appears over at the end of the novel. She says, "Did Peter mention Bob is coming back.... And his prospects are not too bad.... That may make difficulties." He then tells the reader, "things still had their enchantment"

(214). "Still" suggests that the relationship is afloat but will end after the conclusion of the novel. Templer's description of the "acceptance world" foretells the progression of their relationship and comprises the aspect of metonymic description in the major theme of accurate prediction.

On page 170, Nick discusses the aptness of Templer's phrase:

> Even as a technical definition, it seemed to suggest what we are all doing; not only in business, but in love [and] art... Sometimes the goods are delivered, even a small profit made; sometimes the goods are not delivered, and disaster follows; sometimes the goods are delivered, but the value of the currency is changed. Besides, in another sense, the whole world is the Acceptance World as one approaches thirty; at least some illusions are discarded.

This quote highlights the connection between Templer's description and Nick's coincident acceptance into the two worlds described; it predicts his acceptance into the worlds of love and art. In Nick and Jean's relationship "the goods are delivered, even a small profit made" for a while, but, with the advent of Duport's return, "the goods are delivered, but the value of the currency is changed"(170). Nick's acceptance into the world of art is his business relationship with the novelist St. John Clarke, which developed because of his employment in a firm involved with "the publication of art books" (8). Here, "the goods [the contracted *Art of Horace Isbister*] are not delivered, and disaster follows" (170).

Nick's relationship with Jean fulfills Mrs. Erdleigh's tarotic prognostications from their first meeting, and it follows the course laid out by Templer when he describes the "acceptance world." Their fulfillment constitutes the major theme of accurate prediction in the novel.

©Ashton Verdery, 2001

What is Widmerpool Talking About in His Speech?

Jason Myung

Towards the end of *The Acceptance World*, the third volume of *A Dance to the Music of Time*, Jenkins finds himself at a party honoring his old housemaster, La Bas. There, several of his school friends are present and several "old boys" make speeches regarding their lives. However, as things start to wind down, Widmerpool makes an unwelcome speech that inadvertently causes La Bas to have a stroke, effectively ending the party.

The speech concentrates mainly on the economic situation of the world at the time. The Great Depression, or the "most devastating trade depression in our recorded history" (193) as Widmerpool refers to it, has taken a firm hold on global economies, with many countries reeling in debt.

During Widmerpool's long, boring speech, many people find themselves wanting to yank him off the stage, but when deciphered, his words have great implications. Overall, he states that some of the main problems leading to the Great Depression lay in the British government's horrendous money lending policy, calling it "reckless and inadmissible" (193), while also calling the move from the Gold Standard a bad idea, since it seems to have caused rampant inflation and a significant drop in the financial confidence of the British government.

Overall, one might see the underlying economic themes present throughout the book. We have seen Quiggin's Marxist beliefs displayed at the Templar household, specifically when the group begins to use the Planchette. At the household, an important theme arises of the dialectic: Thesis, Antithesis, Synthesis. Looking at it from a poetic view, these three would refer to creation, destruction, and balance/rebirth. But from an economic viewpoint, the dialectic could very well represent the Business Cycle, or Boom and Bust Cycle. The Cycle refers to economic growth, followed by recession, and then balancing out in preparation for the next boom. Obviously, the world is in the tough, Antithesis stage, or recession/depression stage.

An interesting point to make is that through the ideas Widmerpool displays in his speech, he seems to believe in a Keynesian and fiscal approach to economics. This shows him to be a sort of pioneer, since many economics in the thirties still believed in the classical economic model based on things like perfect competition and such. Widmerpool suggests that governments should regulate domestic prices in order to help end the global depression, "Now if a governmental policy of regulating domestic prices is to be arrived at in this or any other country, the moment assigned to the compilation of the index number which will establish the par of interest and prices must obviously be that at which internal economic conditions are in a condition of relative equilibrium" (193).

During his speech, Widmerpool refers to a "curve drawn on a piece of paper." This curve is critical in understanding the situation of the times. This graph representing the "average ratio of persistence" (193), which is comparable and influenced by the average ratio of progress, shows that England's Gross Domestic Product and Gross National Product are slowly decreasing and contracting. Thus, England's economy is shrinking, a very bad thing. Also, Widmerpool discusses methods in which the government can implement a ceiling and baseline price to bring the rampant inflation under control so that the road to recovery becomes easier with a hard currency that is reliably at a set value. But with this set value, production by suppliers will undoubtedly increase in an attempt to make more capital. Here, the government must also control the rate of production in order to insure that prices go neither too far up nor down. However, once Widmerpool states that, "all that is clear enough" (194) he goes on into an unintelligible rant of terms like "index numbers" and "residual commodities" that make no real sense. Here, Powell seems to be making fun of Widmerpool, or showing him just trying to squeeze his way through this part of the speech, and trying to sound intelligent along the way.

The reader will probably wonder why Widmerpool would make such simple concepts in his speech sound so complicated. Widmerpool himself tries to make it seem simple by saying things like "No one would deny that," "So far so good," and "All that is clear enough" when everything obviously is not clear at all. Now the question remains of whether, being the social and business climber that he is, he is just trying to portray himself as highly intelligent or he really is on top of the economic picture. Only time will tell.

©Jason Myung, 2001

ALL IN THE CARDS: CARTOMANCY IN ACCEPTANCE WORLD
CASSIDY CARPENTER

In *The Acceptance World* Anthony Powell uses several types of divination to foreshadow events in the book. One form of prediction is cartomancy, which is used by Mrs. Erdleigh in the Ufford hotel with Nick and Uncle Giles. By looking at the history and significance of cartomancy and horoscopes, we can discover that Powell was well versed in this complex mysticism. The predictions and proclamations by Mrs. Erdleigh about Nick are based on his horoscope and on specific cards that would have been part of her cartomancy reading.

The card reading is triggered by Nick's interest in Mrs. Erdleigh's opal ring. She readily reveals that she was "born in October" and astrologically falls "under the Scales," which refers the sun horoscope Libra (9). The opal is a symbol of her abilities in divination because as the birthstone for October it "enhances your ability to communicate what is in your heart" ("Opal"). Nick responds with the equally important information that he is an archer (9). This means that he was born sometime in late November or December under the sun sign of Sagittarius. Mrs. Erdleigh uses this knowledge to enhance her predictions, using a normal deck of playing cards rather than Tarot.

Cartomancy uses a fifty-two playing card deck to predict the future. There are thirteen cards in each of the four suits corresponding to the thirteen lunar months in a year. The fifty-two cards correspond to the fifty-two weeks in a year and each house relates to a different element. Hearts signifies water, typically happy cards that involve love and friendship. Clubs correspond to the element of fire and cater towards business, ambition, and achievement. Diamonds, elements of earth, generally relate to career and monetary issues. Spades are elements of air; they signify gossip, challenges, and upsets ("Fortune"). Each of the different numbers and face cards in the deck correspond to specific traits and predictions. Anthony Powell uses this fact to foreshadow events in the book using actual predictions that a card would make.

Mrs. Erdleigh uses her knowledge of Nick's horoscope as a base line for the predictions of cartomancy. Nick is a typical Sagittarius, modest, honest, freedom-loving, blindly optimistic, restless, and intellectual ("Astrology Sagittarius"). A common profession of a Sagittarius is a musician, a fact that prompts Mrs. Erdleigh to ask Nick, "Are you musical?" but when he responds he is not, she assumes that he must then be a writer (14). Her next proclamation, "You live between two words," relates to a comment by Nick two pages before as she is setting up the cards, He asks, "That would be Diamonds, I suppose. Or Clubs?" (12). This seemingly irrelevant comment is very significant when horoscopes are applied to cartomancy. Sagittarius, which includes birthdays from November 22nd to December 21st, is under the house of Diamonds ("Learning"). Capricorn, which is under the house of Clubs, spans birth dates from December 22nd to January 19th ("Learning"). There is only a one-day difference between these two houses. This means that Nick's birthday must be near December 21st, and that he tends to express characteristics of a both a Sagittarius and a Capricorn. I discovered *after* making this conclusion that Anthony Powell was born on December 21st, suggesting that Nick and his author share the same birthday! A noteworthy characteristic of Capricorn that Nick expresses, which may have been true for Powell as well, is the tendency to "make few good friends, but remain intensely loyal" ("Astrology Capricorn").

Mrs. Erdleigh's use of cartomancy builds on horoscopes to predict future events in Nick's life. Though Powell does not cite specific cards in the text, a knowledge of cartomancy can suggest which ones would have created the reading that she gives. First a two of clubs may have been drawn, as Mrs. Erdleigh declares that Nick "must make a greater effort in life" (15). This card is a symbol of a crossroads ("Learning"); Nick "can see that" and will have to make a choice of which path he will choose (15). Appropriately this is followed by a prediction of an important lady "of disparate coloring [and] medium hair... and I think you have run across her once or twice before" (15). This of course refers to Jean Templer. In cartomancy the Queen of Clubs refers to a "dark-haired confidant woman." This card may have been coupled with an Ace of Hearts, three of spades, and King of Spades: each respectively symbolizing, a love interest, "a third person breaking into a relationship somehow," and "a dark-haired ambitious man who is perhaps self-serving" ("Fortune Telling"). Mrs. Erdleigh summarizes these cards by saying that "There seems to be another man interested, too. He might even be a husband. You don't like him much.... In business. Often goes abroad" (15). This King of Spades would be Duport, the third person breaking into his relationship with Jean, an event that has not yet developed at this point in the book. The correlation of Mrs. Erdleigh's predictions to the significance of the cards and later events in the book are undeniable.

After an in-depth focus on love and relationships, the predictions shift to business. Mrs. Erdleigh predicts, "There is a small matter in your business that is going to cause inconvenience... It has to do with an elderly man – and two young ones connected with him" (16). Nick immediately thinks that "she might be en rapport with my firm's growing difficulties with St. John Clarke ... and the young man, of course, St. John's secretary, Mark Members" (16). Two cards are associated with this prediction: first, the eight of clubs, which symbolizes work problems that revolve around jealousy, and secondly, the two of diamonds, which involves a business partnership, a change in relationship, and gossip ("Fortune Telling"). The change in relationship that occurs is between Mark Member and Quiggin, a relationship that Mrs. Erdleigh foresees to be "troublesome" (16). Nick recognizes the validity of her statements so far, saying, "This was all credible enough, including the character sketch, though perhaps not very interesting" (16). Nick may not have found this information alarming, but the implications on this prediction are the change in secretary of St. John Clarke.

Divination plays an important role in *The Acceptance World*. Powell effectively uses very specific details and nuances to foreshadow events in the book. The ancient practice of cartomancy plays an important part in understanding Nick's character based on his horoscope, affirming the future relations he will have with Jean, and predicting the break over St. John Clarke between Members and Quiggin. These very important plot points are expertly set up in the first few pages of this novel. Using cartomancy, Powell is able to give insight into the future life and character of Nick Jenkins.

Sources:

1. "Astrology Online: Capricorn." Michael Thiessen. [http://www.astrology-online.com/capricrn.htm]. 6 Nov. 2007.
2. "Astrology Online: Sagittarius." Michael Thiessen. [http://www.astrology-online.com/sagittar.htm]. 6 Nov. 2007.
3. "Fortune Telling Playing Cards: It's All in the Cards." CafeAstrology.com. [http://www.cafeastrology.com/fortunetellingcards.html]. Nov. 6, 2007.
4. "Learning Cartomancy." *Linda*. 6 Nov. 2007 [http://www.geocities.com/canje123/cartomancy1.html]. 6 Nov. 2007.
5. "Opal Gemstone Meaning." *Emily Gems*. [http://crystal-cure.com/opal-gem.html]. Nov. 6, 2007.

To Be, or Not to Be: Attitudes Towards Homosexuality
Michael Donelan

Homosexuality is a pertinent topic in the third novel, *The Acceptance World*, one on which Peter Templer and Nick Jenkins share different views. When Templer sees Nick in the lobby of the Ritz alone, he supposes Nick is waiting for "some ripe little piece" (36), but their brief exchange leads Nick to reply (honestly) that he is waiting for a man, namely Mark Members. Templer quips, "Things have come to that, have they?"

This off-hand comment draws upon Templer's homophobia, which can be traced, back to the beginning of *A Question of Upbringing* when Ackworth tried to pass him a "note" confessing his love for Templer. We already know Nick does not regard homosexuality in any negative light, as he has attended numerous parties of Mr. Deacon's, who is gay, and he has sex with Gypsy who has shown lesbian tendencies according to Mr. Deacon: "I was given to understand -well, hasn't Swinburne got some lines about 'wandering watery sighs where the sea sobs round Lesbian promontories?'" (*BM*, 113).

Templer's unexpected meeting with Nick in the lobby of the Ritz leads not only to the joking comment that Nick is waiting for a male partner, but also leads to the two discussing the film *Mädchen in Uniform*. Templer says that the movie is about lesbians, but Nick repeatedly refutes this view. During their discussion Templer notes, "I couldn't face [*Mädchen in Uniform*]. After all, one meets quite enough lesbians in real life without going to the pictures to see them" (42). This is revealing in that Templer believes there are so many lesbians, and transitively, too many gays that it would be a waste of one's time and money to go see a film made about the subject of homosexuality.

Jenkins, on the other hand, is more open to the idea of homosexuality. He makes friends readily with Mr. Deacon and while he doesn't get along as well with Gypsy Jones socially as he does sexually, he is still able to tolerate her. His open-mindedness leads him to take a more liberal stance on the topic. In the conversation he has with Templer regarding the picture, he claims, "It isn't about lesbians" (42). Because he is so accepting of the idea of homosexuality, he sees the more universal idea of the movie, which is love, regardless of the fact it is between two women.

We see further evidence of Nick's liberal attitude when speaking of Eleanor Walpole-Wilson. Even though we do not have any clear evidence from the text so far, it has been implied that she does not particularly enjoy the company of men and the dances where she would interact with them. We will eventually see she settles down with a partner of the same sex in the countryside, which should not bother Nick at all, due to his relaxed attitude towards homosexuality.

A third woman whom Nick does not look down upon due to her sexual preferences is Mona, Templer's wife. Mona is introduced into *A Buyer's Market* as "a friend of Gypsy's belonging ... to a stage of Gypsy's life before she was known to Mr. Deacon" (*BM* 242). At Mrs. Andriadis's party Members remarks, "She really hates men." (*BM* 243) While it can be inferred that she has had sexual encounters with Gypsy and may be a lesbian, Nick makes no further fuss about the matter. Even much later when Templer and Jenkins are talking about *Mädchen in Uniform* and Templer says Mona will be "disappointed" if it's not about lesbians, Nick does not have any issue with the subject being brought up. Incidentally, we never hear if Templer has any knowledge of Mona's days with Gypsy.

Nick's positive outlook on homosexuality may be misinterpreted as mild ignorance to the untrained eye, especially during discussions of the film. Nick has yet to address the subject himself and never in fact divulges his point of view on this subject. If we look at the series as a whole up to this point we see he allows for some other vehicle to announce the sexual inclinations of Mr. Deacon and Gypsy. Max Pilgrim's song at Milly Andriadis's party infuriates Mr. Deacon, but Nick still does not come out and tell the reader Mr. Deacon is gay. The reader must work hard to uncover this fact through careful analysis of the lyrics. We see that "This verse gave great offence to Mr. Deacon... He was evidently very angry. `Insufferable!' he said. `And from such a person'" (*BM* 118). At the very same party Mr. Deacon recounts a conversation he once had with a man who said `"'Gothic manners don't mix with Greek morals.' Gypsy would never learn that" (*BM* 113).

Homosexuality plays an important role in the unfolding of the plot throughout *The Dance*. We learn a lot during conversations about other people's points of view, but not a lot about Nick's, leading us to believe he is tolerant of gays and lesbians. While this novel may be geared more towards addressing the economics of the 1930's, Nick also addresses the world of love as equal for all. One might say it is an accepting world.

©Michael Donelan, 2007

CHAPTER 4:
AT LADY MOLLY'S

Compared to the first three, *At Lady Molly's* was a harder novel for the students to read, and harder for me to teach. As Nick Jenkins, now fully in the adult world, prepares to marry Isobel Tolland, he leaves their direct experience behind. (Marriage was a consideration for very few – if any – of my students.) The laborious process of sorting out the Tolland family has to happen, too. For a long time not much seems to be happening.

This is not to say there are no events in the novel to capture their interest. They were alive to the comedy of Widmerpool's romance, and Nick's wonderful line, "It may surprise you to hear that when I embark on clandestine week-ends, I call myself 'Widmerpool'" (61). In her essay Kym Louie struggles mightily with the enigmatic nature of his sexual drive. We all discussed at length Nick's remarkable paragraph on page 136, where he talks about his instantaneous realization that he will marry Isobel, but no one wrote about it.

For this book most of them chose to analyze characters: General Conyers, Ted Jeavons, Erridge, Nick himself, and – of course – Widmerpool. In addition to Kym's essay, I've included Nathaniel Miller on Erridge and Jake Bean's remarkable analogy of matter/anti-matter in reference to those two military forces, General Conyers and Uncle Giles. Finally Kim Sugerman did some research on the "quota quickies" in Britain, discovering some interesting material on Powell himself.

SYNOPSIS

At Lady Molly's begins in London around the New Year of 1934. Jenkins, now working as a scriptwriter, is invited to a party at Lady Molly Jeavons's by his colleague, Chips Lovell. He recalls a childhood meeting with Mrs. Conyers, an old family friend and wife of General Conyers, and her sister, Mildred. At Lady Molly's he encounters Mrs. Conyers and discovers that the party is being held for her sister Mildred, now Haycock, now in her 40's, and her new fiancé, Widmerpool.

Lunching at his club with Jenkins, Widmerpool asks advice about a premarital weekend with Mildred Haycock. Then Jenkins goes to tea with General and Mrs. Conyers, joined by Frederica Tolland Budd, all of whom ask about Widmerpool. Frederica gives him a lift, and they stop in to see Norah Tolland and Eleanor Walpole-Wilson. Finally Jenkins goes to a movie with an unnamed date; on the way in, they encounter Quiggin.

Jenkins goes to visit Quiggin and Mona at their home, which turns out to be a guest cottage at Thrubworth, the Tollands' estate. They all go to visit Erridge for dinner. There Erridge and Quiggin discuss the financing of a planned magazine. Isobel and Susan arrive, and we learn of Susan's engagement to Roddy Cutts. Jenkins believes he will marry Isobel. The butler Smith's alcoholism is discovered, and we begin to see Mona's flirting with Erridge.

Lovell describes Jeavons to Jenkins before they go to Molly's. There, Nick sees Miss Weedon, who is looking after Stringham. He leaves Molly's with Jeavons, who takes him to a club run by Dicky Umfraville. Templer arrives with Widmerpool, Mildred Haycock, and Templer's date, a woman named Betty. Max Pilgrim and Heather Hopkins perform. Jeavons reveals to Nick that during the war he spent a weekend with Mildred. Widmerpool goes home ill, but Mildred and Jeavons recognize each other and remain. At the end of the chapter Nick states that he "too, should be married soon enough."

Jenkins visits with Lady Katherine Warminster and discusses Erridge and Mona's trip to China. Later, Lady Molly holds a party in honor of Jenkins's engagement to Isobel. At the party, Jenkins talks to Members, as well as General Conyers. The General pulls Jenkins aside, and eagerly tells him about Widmerpool's inability to perform sexually with Mildred. Widmerpool arrives at the end, seemingly unaffected by the cancellation of his wedding.

CHARACTER LIST

These are the major characters in this volume. Although they are mostly organized by chapter, members the Tolland family (who appear *passim* throughout the volume) are listed first, in order of their birth:

The Tollands

Alfred T., Lord Erridge, Earl of Warminster (called "Erry") – eldest brother, in his thirties, an eccentric, left-leaning peer
Frederica T. Budd – distinguished, a Lady-in-Waiting
Norah T. – a lesbian, living with Eleanor Walpole-Wilson
George T. – was at school with Jenkins
Blanche T. – "dotty," does good works
Susan T. – about 25 or 26, becomes engaged to Roddy Cutts
Robert T. - in business, "a bit of a mystery"
Isobel T. – "highbrow," goes to nightclubs, becomes engaged to Jenkins
Hugo T. – at university, somehow "unsatisfactory"
Pricilla T. – not "out" yet, Chips Lovell's interest

Chapter 1

Chips Lovell – scriptwriter, colleague and friend of Jenkins
General Conyers – Jenkins's family friend, eccentric, military hero
Bertha (Blaides) Conyers – his wife
Mildred Blaides (later Haycock) – Bertha's sister, a nurse, "rackety"
Lady Molly (Ardglass) Sleaford Jeavons – aunt of the Tolland children, giver of informal parties
Ted Jeavons – Molly's husband, mild-mannered, not aristocratic
Uncle Alfred Tolland – uncle of the Tolland children
Smith – Erridge's dreadful butler, sometimes helps Lady Molly
Widmerpool – engaged to Mildred Haycock

Chapter 2

Eleanor Walpole-Wilson – old friend, living with Norah Tolland
Heather Hopkins – neighbor of Eleanor and Norah, piano player
J. G. Quiggin – Marxist critic, friend of Jenkins since university

Chapter 3

Mona – Templer's ex-wife, presently living with Quiggin

Chapter 4

Tuffy Weedon – woman looking after Stringham
Mrs. Foxe – Stringham's mother
Dicky Umfraville – nightclub owner, knew Stringham in Kenya
Max Pilgrim – a gay entertainer

WIDMERPOOL'S ROMANCES
KYM LOUIE

From the time Jenkins meets Widmerpool at school, Widmerpool is socially awkward and continually trying to fit in. Jenkins does not even consider the possibility of his having an interest in a woman until he confesses his feelings for Barbara. Jenkins says, "somehow I had never been able to picture his life as an adult; idly fancying him, if thought of at all, forever floundering towards the tape in races never won" (*BM* 30). Though Widmerpool races toward women, he does not win them either. In fact he does not seem very interested in having romantic relationships with women, except to appear normal in society.

The first time Jenkins sees Widmerpool take an interest in a woman is at the ball at the Huntercombes'. At the time, "Widmerpool still represented in my mind a kind of embodiment of thankless labour and unsatisfied ambition" (*BM* 30). He is supposed to dance with Barbara when she insists on leaving the dance floor with Jenkins, Widmerpool and Tompsitt. He is "by no means prepared to give in at once, though his struggles to keep Barbara to himself were feeble enough, and quite ineffectual" (*BM* 66). Widmerpool is outraged at this, but makes no show of it. Later that night, he grabs Barbara's wrist to prevent her from leaving. Here Jenkins notes that Widmerpool had always been "inclined to shrink from physical contact," and while in France had "started violently [as she touched his arm], almost as if Berthe's plump fingers were red-hot" (*BM* 69). Widmerpool's action is not one of adoration nor affection; he is clearly only trying to prevent her from leaving him for the evening. He reacts to Barbara's pouring sugar over his head with a fury clearly from humiliation, not from disappointment in the prospect of her showing no romantic interest in him. Jenkins reflects that he "used to think that people who looked and behaved like Widmerpool had really no right to fall in love at all" (*BM* 80). Widmerpool and Jenkins leave the ball and immediately run into Gypsy Jones and Mr. Deacon.

Widmerpool does not take an immediate interest in Gypsy, but as the night wears on, he becomes more and more attentive to her. Gypsy herself turns out not to be actively pursuing a romantic relationship, as she later reveals that Widmerpool paid for her abortion simply because "somebody had to cough up" (*BM* 249). Jenkins sees nothing in Gypsy that he expects to be particularly attractive to Widmerpool, but thinks that he might take a fancy to her "on the rebound" (*BM* 249) from Barbara. Despite the major differences between the two women, Nick notices that they share a kind of "sociological preoccupation." Widmerpool certainly is not very sociable himself, nor is he interested in spending large amounts of time at social activities, so he is not interested in anything long-term with either of the women.

However, if he were to go out with one of them, he would be seen as socially successful. Jenkins later finds out from General Conyers that Widmerpool is incapable of performing sexually with his fiancée, so it is unlikely that in the case of Gypsy there was any physical relationship between the two. He only provides an abortion for Gypsy, which he calls "an almost insanely indiscreet thing about the girl you introduced me to (*BM* 207)," showing that it he does not have feelings for her strong enough to justify his actions and the amount of money it costs him.

Jenkins does not report Widmerpool having any more relationships with women until he learns of his engagement to Mildred Blaides. She, like Barbara and Gypsy, is a socialite, although she is an older one. Widmerpool tells Jenkins of his plans to go with her to Dogdene, showing how analytical he is being about the entire relationship, and that the two of them have most probably not been physically intimate at all. General Conyers describes his behavior there:

> Half the time he was being obsequious, behaving as
> if he was applying for the job as a footman, the other

> half, he was telling Geoffrey Sleaford and myself how
> to run our own affairs.... It was with Mildred there
> was some awkwardness.... The fact was, Mildred did
> not think he was paying her enough attention (229).

This shows that Widmerpool is not very interested in Mildred, even though she is his fiancée. Furthermore, he is unable to perform sexually with her. Thus, when she calls off the wedding, he is anything but devastated. He may actually be relieved at this turn of events, because, as Nick notes throughout the books, Widmerpool is awkward and uncomfortable around women. Though having a wife may make him appear more professional, his relief at his separation with Mildred suggests that being close to a woman is by far not his top priority.

Initially Widmerpool appears to Jenkins as undeserving of any relationships with women, and, as time progresses, he acts as if they mean nothing to him. His relationships, or lack thereof, with Barbara, Gypsy, and Mildred show that he is only interested in being close with women publicly, and the actual relationships mean little to him.

©Kym Louie, 2007

GENERAL CONYERS: THE ANTI-UNCLE GILES
JACOB BEAN

In cosmology, antimatter is defined as matter composed of antiparticles that, upon colliding with a matching particle of normal matter, annihilate and convert the mass of both particles into energy. In Anthony Powell's *Dance to the Music of Time* a similar reaction might be expected in a collision between Uncle Giles and General Conyers. Conyers is worldly and unpredictable while Uncle Giles remains bitter and unchanging. Just as an antiproton is the opposite of a proton and a positron is the opposite of an electron so General Conyers is the opposite of Uncle Giles.

The first description of General Conyers in the opening pages of *At Lady Molly's* highlights many of the differences between him and Uncle Giles. Nick describes General Conyers as "a man of the world, always 'abreast of the times,'" with a "taste for being in fashion and giving his opinion on every subject" – a reputation "held against him by ... Uncle Giles" (1) Already a clear distinction is apparent between the two characters: Conyers the "man of the world" and Giles "no friend of up-to-date thought, and on principal suspicious of worldly success" (1). Contrary to Uncle Giles, Conyers "always knew the right people." He is "fond of dressing himself up to the nines"(1). He was known to "chase the women a bit"(3) during the war, though Uncle Giles, we know, has had his own affairs of the heart; "his first serious misadventure ... had, indeed, centred upon a love affair" (*QU* 64). Conyers has had a successful military career reaching the rank of brigadier-general and was "expected to go much further" before he "married a woman nearly twenty years younger than himself"(3). Although he isn't very good, "he had always loved playing the 'cello" and occupies much of his time "experimenting with a favorite theory that poodles, owning to their keen natural intelligence, could profitably be trained as gun dogs"(4). Married life hasn't slowed him down and he maintains a "rather social life"(4).

The first descriptions of Uncle Giles are quite contrary to those of General Conyers. Uncle Giles is described as "neat, and still slightly military in appearance"(16), in spite of the fact that he "had not held a commission for at least twenty years"(16). Contrary to General Conyers', Uncle Giles has had a lackluster army career. "Captain was probably a more or less honorary rank"(16). He didn't particularly enjoy his time in the military, and in fact it was one of his "chief complaints that he had been `put' into the army," a career "for which he possessed neither Mrs. Foxe's romantic admiration or her hard-headed grasp of military realities"(64). His departure from service was a dishonorable affair; though there was never a court-martial, "the necessity for [him] to turn in his papers was unquestioned"(65).

While General Conyers "always knew the right people," Uncle Giles suffered from what he called a "lack of influence," an attribute "which he invested, to a greater or lesser degree, every human being on earth except himself"(66). When he did seem to know people they often turned out to be "undesirable friends"(65). While both Conyers and Giles chase women, Conyers is the only one who seems to have had success. One of the most evident differences between the two characters is Conyers's ability to change unexpectedly while Uncle Giles remains fixed, a constant to which Nick can draw comparisons. After meeting his soon-to-be wife, General Conyers promptly, and "much to the surprise of his friends – married a woman nearly twenty years younger than himself; sending in his papers about eighteen months later"(3). This was a rather unexpected alteration in his life, which nevertheless General Conyers accepted without missing a beat. Uncle Giles, on the other hand, seems incapable of making such a radical change and seems doomed to forever squabble over his share of the trust.

Antimatter, while admittedly strange, does serve a purpose. When it collides with its counterpart it creates energy, energy that can fuel production. So if General Conyers is the foil to Uncle

Giles, then what is his purpose? It seems that the consistency of Uncle Giles has allowed him to become a meter-stick, a tool to be used by Nick to measure others. General Conyers' role is a little less clear. At the end of the fourth book he provides useful information regarding the break up of Widmerpool and Mildred, information we might not have encountered otherwise. However, whether he will take a larger role in Nick's life in the subsequent novels remains to be seen.

Source:

Seeds, Michael A. *Horizons Exploring the Universe*. 8th ed. Brooks/Cole, 2004.

©Jacob Bean, 2007

ERRIDGE: ARISTOCRAT, COMMUNIST, AND ECCENTRIC
NATHANIEL MILLER

In Anthony Powell's *At Lady Molly's* the narrator, Nick Jenkins, meets many members of the Tolland family, including Alfred Tolland, Earl of Warminster. From his title he owns a large manor house, Thrubworth Park, as well as much of the surrounding land, and holds a peerage in the House of Lords. He also possesses an extraordinary streak of eccentricities. He uses only a fraction of his house, which is minimally staffed. His appearance is disheveled. Politically he is a communist, interested in land redistribution. He decides to steal away to the Far East. In summary, he is a driven aristocratic peer, with an eccentric personality, a combination that leads him from a stuffy and grand, if unkempt, manor house to an almost comic adventure to the Far East. What is expected of the earl, a stable life built on his inheritance of a peerage, stands in sharp contrast to his eccentric politics and dealings.

As the eldest of his generation of Tollands, Alfred Tolland became Viscount Erridge upon his grandfather's death, signifying that he would inherit the title of Earl of Warminster when his father died, along with Thrubworth Park, a peerage, and all the other privileges of that title. His family continues to call him "Erridge" or "Erry" in reference to this first title. When he does become Earl of Warminster, he does little with his inheritance, preferring to live in a very small portion of the house, while the rest remains "under dust sheets" (151). At the same time, Erridge greatly enjoys showing guests around the house, and knows a great deal of family history. There are only a few employees at Thrubworth Park, most prominently a cranky, drunkard butler, Smith, and he is often loaned out. Chips Lovell mentions that his aunt Molly, the title character, "sometimes borrows him from Erridge, when, for one reason or another, Thrubworth is closed down" (21). Erridge's title, Earl of Warminster, also entitles him to a seat in the House of Lords, although the power such a seat commanded would have waned considerably by the 1930s.

The British nobility were still able to wield considerable influence, however, with much of it coming from the large yearly income a title guaranteed. If Erridge uses much of his income, he does so in the service of various communist causes. The Marxist literary critic J.G. Quiggin mentions that Erridge has, "founded several societies and financed them … All very good causes … But sums that would make you gasp" (154). When Erridge first appears in person, he and Quiggin are making plans to start a political magazine, as well as to publish some anti-fascist pamphlets. According to Quiggin, it is also Erridge's intention to turn Thrubworth Park, "into a collective farm with himself at the head of it" (115). This is also a subtle rebuke of Erridge's reluctance to give up power, which he would have to do in a truly Marxist society. At this point, Erridge has just returned from a committee meeting on the Sedition Bill in London, which was aborted due to the absence of another important member of the committee.

Erridge's influential, almost ironically executive, presence in British communism contrasts with a determination to be like working people in many ways. He does not bother with his appearance or clothes, which are described by Nick as giving off, "a heavy, earthen smell as if he had lived out of them in all weathers for a long time" (115). Quiggin informs Nick that Erridge has been, "collecting useful information about unemployment," (123) and distributing pamphlets. However, these eccentricities are insignificant in comparison with Erridge's most astonishing decision: to travel overseas to the Far East in order to see the conditions in China during the Japanese invasion. This would not have been notable in and of itself because, as Nick notes, he was, "interested in the political implications of the situation" and, "could afford to buy a ticket for himself" (204); however, at this time Erridge decides to leave Quiggin behind and travel with only Mona. Not only does this seriously threaten Erridge's relationship with Quiggin, it throws his family into a speculative turmoil.

In many ways Erridge's trip to the Far East captures the essence of his character. Just when his position seems completely outrageous, a communist aristocrat personally collecting data on unemployment, he goes even farther afield by running for the conflict-ridden Far East with Mona in tow. His life shifts from the merely incongruous to the absurd in his, so far, short appearance. He seems to have no logical progression in his oddities. For example, the Far East journey was first suggested by Quiggin.

At the same time, Erridge seems to do take little action without some sort of purpose. When he visits Quiggin's house, he does not care what he interrupts in order to bring up his magazine. He does things his own way, such as setting up water pumps in all the houses on his property, and is used to his own power and influence. He is willing to leave behind the comforts of an aristocratic life in order to achieve his goals. All this leads to his decision to temporarily abandon life at Thrubworth Park for the Far East, once again in sharp contrast with outside expectations, in order to chart his own, eccentric journey in life.

©Nathaniel Miller, 2007

Quota Quickies:
The British Film Quota, Nick, and Powell
Kim Sugerman

In the beginning of *At Lady Molly's* by Anthony Powell, the reader is given a glance into Nick's life as a film writer. He continues to mention his profession throughout the book, getting different receptions. Nick's story is similar to that of Powell's own life. Both wrote film scripts, an opportunity that probably would not have occurred without "the quota." As American movies came to dominate the film industry in England, the government required that for every American movie shown, a certain number of British films had to be played. The American movies were more popular, so the British government set up a ratio for the quota in order to protect their own film industry. As a result, many writers wound up working for film companies, changing British film forever.

The British film quota was created in 1927 when Parliament passed the Cinematograph Films Act. At the time, the British cinema culture was growing, helped by the founding of The Film Society of London in 1925 and more reviews in the papers. Movies are mentioned in *Dance* several times such as when Mona and Jean go to the film that Templer believes is "about lesbians." Nick takes part in the increasing popularity of movies, mentioning that he often stands in a film queue with different girls.

American film was being exported in large amounts at this time, and was beginning to dominate the film scene. In 1925, Britain only produced 33 films. In 1926, more than 600 American films were shown in England. Since the movies had already made a profit in the United States, they were cheap to go see. As a result of the influx of American films, the quota was enacted and many English writers, actors, and directors were given jobs. American corporations such as Paramount, Warner Brothers, and Fox set up subsidiaries in England to produce cheap films.

A film counted as British if at least 75 percent of the salaries went to citizens of Britain, including the writer ("In Praise"). It also had to be produced in the United Kingdom. Since these films had to be produced quickly, they were often of poor quality and did not require large investments. They gained the title of "quota quickies," which is still used to describe low-quality movies made during the 1930s. Often these movies were produced for less than £1 per foot; one producer was able to complete an entire film for this price in ten days. This is the type of team that Nick mentions in his story. He, Chips Lovell, Hegarty, and Feingold had already produced nine "treatments" between them, even though they had been in the industry only a short time. As a result, these films could be quite boring, but they sometimes provided an outlet for more unusual plots. Others were very successful and, since the filmmakers did not have to pay the stars very much, it was easier to make a profit. In fact some were indistinguishable from the costlier productions. One actor said that they often filmed the films at a country house the producer was using for vacation, often without rehearsals.

When Nick goes to visit Quiggin and Mona at their cottage, it becomes apparent that the reason for the invitation is to discuss Mona's prospects as a film star. This is very optimistic of the couple because Nick wrote only for the quota, working for a company that produced second-feature films, which did not use major stars. Quiggin mentions that Mona "has made more than one appearance on the screen in the past" (110). However, Nick replies that it will be difficult for him to introduce her to any directors since he is on the scenario side. He tells Ted Jeavons that he has "little to no contact with the acting side of the business" (111).

Nick says that "to be 'an author' was, of course a recognized path of approach to this means of livelihood; so much so, indeed, at that period, that to serve a term as a script-writer was almost a routine stage in literary life" (12). However, Widmerpool takes a different view, commenting on Nick's "unusual ways ... to earn a living." When Widmerpool inquires whether he likes the work, he replies curtly, "Not greatly" (52), and receives the familiar reply that it might lead to something better. Nick has previously written several novels and writing for films is a good way to keep working during the Slump. However, people in the film industry were often paid very little; one company "never paid more than £150 to a screenwriter, or £250 to a star" (Sweet). He had to work long hours, as evidenced by his staying late regularly with Lovell.

Anthony Powell worked for Warner Brothers Studio in Teddington (Sweet). He was a scriptwriter – a similar position to Nick's – who helped write the second feature. Also similar to Nick's job, his hours were long, but they paid fairly well. Powell's contract expired after six months and was not renewed, and none of his scripts was ever turned into a movie.

However, the film quota was an important part of British film history. Without the ability to mass-produce films, many of the actors and directors never would have gained the experience that made them famous in later years. The quota was success as more and more people went to watch British films. Eventually the quota act changed to improve the quality of the films by requiring a certain amount of money be spent on each foot of film, and British film became even more popular.

Sources:

1. "Great Britain: Quotas, Quota Quickies, and Sound." *Film Reference.* http://www.filmreference.com. 11 Dec 2007.
2. "In Praise of the Quota." *British Pictures.* http://www. britishpicutres.com. 10 Dec 2007.
3. Sweet, Matthew. "Fancy a Quickie?" *The Guardian.* 2 Jan 2007 http://www.film.guardian.co.uk. 11 Dec 2007.

CHAPTER 5:
CASANOVA'S CHINESE RESTAURANT

I have always been fascinated by *Casanova's Chinese Restaurant.* First of all, the opening is so complicated, with its flashbacks and flashforwards, that – although there's no doubt about what Jenkins is telling us about Moreland – we have to scramble, and test, and eventually argue to figure out when the various events in the first chapter take place.

Then there's the character of Hugh Moreland, who casts a great brilliance over the rest of the series. I showed the class that Powell introduces him *post mortem*, and that the opening section is a sort of eulogy for him – a bow towards the future (since his death won't happen for five more volumes) that happens nowhere else in *Dance.* With Moreland Nick at last has a friend on whom he can rely for conversation, for bonhomie, for support. Both Stringham and Templer have proven unreliable, but Moreland – as difficult as he may make his own life – never seems to stop enjoying Nick's company. And with Moreland, the series can at last address the art of music in England in the first half of the 20th century.

This was also the first volume of the second term, and we had new readers to introduce to *Dance.* I have included a piece by Alyssa Warren, who writes thoughtfully of the problems – and the advantages – she discovered when entering the series here. Most interesting to me is her assessment of Erridge; clearly, we do not read each new volume free from the biases of the volumes that have come before.

Other essays raise other issues from the novel. Corey Simpson finally addresses the sometimes exasperating narrative voice of Nick Jenkins, who tells us so little of himself. John Bukawyn considers the case of Tuffy Weedon. And Katherine Cascio writes the first of a pair of interdisciplinary papers I'm including. Her mother is a psychologist, and Katherine was taking psychology at the same time as "The Longest Novel Ever Written." She applies her theories to Maclintick – who certainly could benefit from them. She will use them again in two volumes to show a relationship between Maclintick and another, most unlikely character.

————————— SYNOPSIS —————————

Casanova's Chinese Restaurant opens after World War II at the bombed-out site of the Mortimer, a pub Jenkins used to go to. Through a series of recollections, we see Jenkins meet Hugh Moreland, a composer, in the late 20s. Through him and Mr. Deacon, Jenkins meets Maclintick, Carolo, and Gossage, all three associated with music, and Norman Chandler, a dancer. Later in the evening they dine with Barnby. Jumping to the mid-30s, Jenkins attends a play with Moreland and meets his girlfriend, Matilda Wilson, an actress. At the play he meets Mark Members, Stringham's mother Mrs. Foxe, and Chandler. Finally we learn that Matilda and Moreland marry, about a year before Jenkins and Isobel do.

Members of the Tolland family attend luncheon at Katherine, Lady Warminister's, where Jenkins finds out that Erridge has gone to Spain to support the Leftists in its civil war. St. John Clarke also is present; Erridge has left him in charge of Thrubworth, which is in serious financial difficulties. Jenkins then visits Isobel, who is in a nursing home because of a miscarriage, and while there he runs into Moreland (whose wife is pregnant) and Widmerpool (who has boils). Jenkins goes with Moreland to Maclintick's house. The Maclinticks fight during the whole visit, leaving Jenkins and Moreland uncomfortable. A few days later Jenkins eats lunch with Widmerpool.

The Morelands' daughter dies shortly after birth. A year or two later Mrs. Foxe, helped by Norman Chandler, throws a party for Moreland, in honor of a new symphony. At the party, the Maclinticks fight; Matilda reveals to Nick that she and Carolo were once married and that Moreland and Pricilla have "something on." Stringham appears, drunk but funny, and charms Mrs. Maclintick, but is taken away when Commander Foxe phones Tuffy Weedon, his caretaker. The Morelands leave the party separately, as does Pricilla.

Mrs. Maclintick leaves her husband to go off with Carolo. Jenkins and Moreland visit Maclintick trying to cheer him up, but a few days later he gasses himself. Moreland tells Jenkins that the affair with Pricilla is over. Robert announces that Pricilla is marrying Chips Lovell, and Frederica announces that St. John Clarke has left his fortune to Erridge, who thus will not have to sell Thrubworth Woods to solve the financial difficulties.

CHARACTER LIST

The major characters in this volume, arranged by chapter:

Chapter 1

Hugh Moreland – composer, Jenkins's best friend
Ralph Barnby – a painter, a friend of Jenkins and Mr. Deacon
Mr. Deacon – elderly friend of Jenkins, owns an antique shop
Maclintick – a music reviewer
Gossage – another music critic
Carolo – a violinist
Norman Chandler – a dancer and actor
Mrs. Foxe – Stringham's rich, aristocratic mother
Mark Members – a writer, university friend of Jenkins
Matilda Wilson – an actress, love interest of Moreland

Chapter 2

Widmerpool – businessman, at school with Jenkins
Dr. Brandreth – physician for Widmerpool and Matilda
St. John Clarke – an older writer
Lady Warminster – the Tollands' stepmother
Frederica, Hugo, Robert, Blanche, George, Susan, Pricilla – various Tollands, Jenkins's in-laws
Chips Lovell – works with Jenkins
Veronica – George's wife
Roddy Cutts – Susan's husband, a member of Parliament
Audrey Maclintick – Maclintick's awful wife

Chapter 3

Eleanor Walpole-Wilson – lives with Norah Tolland
Commander Foxe ("Buster") – Stringham's stepfather
Lady and Lord Huntercombe – rich patrons of the arts
Miss Weedon ("Tuffy") – Stringham's caretaker
Charles Stringham – Jenkins's old school friend, now alcoholic

Chapter 4

J. G. Quiggin – a writer, a staunch Marxist

Entering the Dance: A Newcomer's Reflection
Alyssa Warren

As one of the few students entering the class in the winter term, I began reading *Dance to the Music of Time* with *Casanova's Chinese Restaurant*. Delving into this epic novel one-third of the way through has confronted me with a seemingly disadvantageous viewpoint. With each new chapter, references to past events elude me and I am forced to depend on my classmates' interpretations of these scenes. While I do accept these pieces of information, I cannot help but wish that I could analyze these scenes independently. Beyond inhibiting my ability to analyze events and characters, this deficit of knowledge has caused much of Powell's humor to elude me. I'm beginning now to overcome my frustration. I realize that this seemingly negative experience has given me the innocence to read this book without prejudice. I cannot judge the characters based on their past accomplishments or misdemeanors. This superficial reading grants me, and the few others who have begun the dance partway through, the capacity for honest character judgment. While I still lack key elements of the story, I realize that I can indeed depend on my classmates' insights and recollections as a foundation and still use my innocence to provide a fresh perspective to their readings.

Moreland's post-mortem introduction on the second page did not strike me as anything extraordinary. Unaware that Nick had never introduced a character in this way, I continued reading without an additional thought. During the class discussion following chapter one, an emphasis was placed on this statement: "As an accompaniment to Moreland's memory music was natural, even imperative... (2). The class believed this post-mortem introduction to be significant and thus spent a large portion of time wondering why Moreland's character justified such a grand entrance. Even after learning that this type of introduction had never happened before, I could not grasp its significance. I continued reading and learning about Moreland based solely on his actions and dialogue throughout the novel and without hype about him. As the story progresses, Moreland does become a prominent character as one of Jenkins's close friends. Simultaneously, however, he does not represent a great man or seem to possess a higher morality than the others, as his affair with Priscilla Tolland demonstrates. Perhaps in later novels Moreland's role will develop and his importance will become clearer. Until this point, reading about him without an assumed importance allows me to interpret Moreland's actions without bias and simply observe the development of Jenkins's and his friendship.

As the story continues, much of Powell's subtle humor sneaks past me, unnoticed and underappreciated. This dampens my overall reading experience and creates a feeling of being excluded. As if I am on the outside of a group of old friends and acquaintances, I feel uninterested at times. Most notably, I recall reading quickly past the section of Mr. Deacon's remarks regarding Norman Chandler's sexual orientation. Mr. Deacon relays the information that "another theatrical friend ... rather a naughty young man" will be arriving at the Mortimer shortly for a business deal (17). Later in this chapter references to Max Pilgrim and Norman Chandler's friendship do not outwardly suggest a romantic connection. Without the previous knowledge of Mr. Deacon and Max Pilgrim's homosexuality, I simply regarded these characters as names and, lacking background, I did not attempt to infer more about their characters. This particular incident did not hinder my understanding of the story; however, I missed Powell's intended wit.

Perhaps slightly less amused with the happenings of *Casanova's Chinese Restaurant* than my classmates and certainly less informed regarding the characters, I read on to meet Erridge. He faces brutal ridicule from the other characters and serves as the subject of many satirical remarks, which may affect the reader's perception of him. The class introduced him to the newcomers as the "screw-up" of the Tolland family, the son who journeys off to the Far East with Mona, and the son who struggles to manage his estate. Priscilla Tolland states simply, "Erry is mad, of course" (70). As always, I listened and accepted, though somewhat hesitantly, this information. Continuing the reading, I found myself drawn to Erridge's political passion, pacifistic sentiment, and bravery. "Devoting himself to his leftwing political interests," Erridge ventures to Spain to support his fellow liberal activists and soldiers in the Spanish Civil War (59). This deed demonstrates not only his political conviction but also his courage in actually backing up his rhetoric with action. I further respect Erridge for his traveling, perhaps as means for expanding his global perspective, and for having the strength to live a socially isolated life at Thrubworth.

Through my limited experience of this novel, I have learned that viewing my late start as a disadvantage might further reduce the potential influence this novel can have on me. Open-mindedness will benefit my future readings. My innocence, slowly diminishing as I read, grants me the clarity of mind to make fair judgments and offer a fresh perspective to the class. Although I have learned to call Powell "pole" and not "pow-ell" and to read St. John Clarke as "singeonclark," I am still far from accustomed to the world of Nick Jenkins and am yet to feel as if his friends are my own acquaintances. However, as I continue reading further into Powell's epic novel, my initial "disadvantage" continues to disappear, allowing the events and characters of the story to imprint a literary experience in my memory.

©Alyssa Warren, 2008

None of Your Business: Nick's Selective Narration
Corey Simpson

As a narrator, Nick Jenkins observes his acquaintances with a critical eye. Even when he does not offer an opinion, the specific anecdotes and dialogues he shares invite the readers to analyze the characters for themselves, and his choice of what information to provide subtly guides the reader to view people the same way that Nick does. However, Nick tends to neglect the topics that one would think would be the most important; anything the reader learns about Nick's personal life is a bare minimum of background information required to further the plot, and nothing more. It is almost as if Nick avoids all mention of his home life because he does not want the readers to analyze and judge it in the same way they do the other characters; Nick's acquaintances are fair game, but his family is none of our business.

The details of Nick's marriage to his wife, Isobel, are the most noticeable of all the information Nick withholds. *Casanova's Chinese Restaurant* marks the first time we see Nick as a married man, and yet his wife is hardly mentioned, and speaks only a few sentences in the course of the entire book. Although they have technically become a part of Nick's family, he continues to discuss the Tollands; he became interested in the eccentric clan long before he met Isobel, and is not close enough to any of them to warrant the kind of reticence that his immediate family inspires. In recounting his visit to their house in Chapter 2, Nick is forced to include their inquiries about Isobel's health, but he at first refuses to elaborate and gives far more attention to other, more trivial topics. Indeed, he responds to all the questions about Isobel with almost the exact same phrase; first "Pretty well all right now. She is emerging tomorrow. I am going to see her this afternoon" (62) and later "Pretty well all right now. I am going to see her this afternoon." (70) In the face of the curiosity sparked by the Tollands' concern, Nick's mechanical replies are maddening.

Later, however, when Nick visits the nursing home, he grants us an insight into his reluctance to discuss his wife. He says:

> It is doubtful whether an existing marriage can ever be described directly in the first person and convey a sense of reality. Even those writers who suggest some of the substance of married life best, stylise heavily, losing the subtlety of the relationship at the price of a few accurately recorded, but isolated, aspects. To think at all objectively about one's own marriage is impossible, while a balanced view of other people's marriage is almost equally hard to achieve with so much information available, so little to be believed. Objectivity is not, of course, everything in writing; but even casting objectivity aside, the difficulties of presenting a marriage are inordinate.... Marriage ... defies definition. (97)

Nick does not feel that writing is really sufficient to convey his feelings about Isobel, so he doesn't even try. He also reaffirms his reluctance to allow the readers to pass judgment on his personal relationships, fearing that they will not maintain a "balanced view" of his marriage. We have known from the beginning that finding love is deeply important to Nick, so much so that he is willing to overlook the most glaring faults if a girl happens to strike his fancy (see the Barbara Goring fiasco). All of his other relationships are different; Nick may like his friends, but he acknowledges their flaws. Nick's feelings for Isobel fit neither the pattern of blind adoration, nor of detached fondness-rather, Nick seems to assume that if he has introduced her as the only girl he has actually wanted to marry, then that should be the end of that.

From this point in the series, we better understand Nick's desire to protect his privacy. It may occasionally be frustrating – we would like to know more about the woman who is so important to our narrator, after all – but the series is intended to be an observation of society set in the context of Nick's life, and from that perspective, his personal affairs really are "none of our business." And while the naturally curious among us would undoubtedly like to know more about the married life of Nick and Isobel, all we really need to know about their relationship is provided in the exchange at the end of their visit in the nursing home; "'I shan't be sorry to come home.' `I shan't be sorry for you to be home again.'" (97)

Tuffy Weedon: Stringham's Keeper

John Bukawyn

Throughout Anthony Powell's *A Dance to the Music of Time*, characters and their roles evolve. Tuffy Weedon's place in the Foxe household changes from that of Stringham's sister's governess to Stringham's babysitter. What remains constant, however, is the fact the she stays a stable source of backing for Stringham; when we first meet her, he comments that she is, "a great supporter of mine" (*QU* 59). From that first meeting in *A Question of Upbringing* to her entrance in *Casanova's Chinese Restaurant*, her notion of support towards Stringham completely transforms.

During the summer after school lets out, Nick pays a visit to Stringham's on his way through London. On this stopover, Stringham introduces Tuffy to Nick and the reader. When she walks into the room, Stringham seems pleased to see her, and she is likewise delighted to see him: "her face took on a sudden look of intensity, almost of anxiety, the look that women's faces sometimes show at a moment of supreme pleasure" (*QU* 58). The fact that they are both happy to see one another suggests that that their relationship is mutual, rather than dominated by one or the other. Indeed her pleasant feelings toward him are noticeable not only in her appearance, but also in her actions because it was she, not his parents, who remembered to purchase him a ticket to the Russian ballet. In an act of friendly concern, she acts for his benefit, so that he may simply enjoy an evening with his family.

The next place we see her is at Oxford, where she gives Stringham a different kind of encouragement. As he prepares to leave the University before taking a degree, Tuffy arrives to advise him in the matter. Sillery, a don at Oxford, is also pushing very hard for Stringham to go down and take a position with Sir Magnus Donners. When Stringham's mother cannot be present, Tuffy replaces her. In this way, she acts maternally when discussing Stringham's future. As if she were defending her own child, she protects him from Sillery's manipulative ways. Sillery immediately tries to establish his importance at the table by name-dropping, trying to control the conversation. He mentions his own acquaintance with "Mr. Gladstone" (the former prime minister). Tuffy counters this by congratulating Stringham on his lunch, saying, "Did you arrange all this lunch yourself...How wonderful of you" (*QU* 214). She talks solely about Stringham and his accomplishments, as if she is his proud mother, praising her child. Replacing his mother for that moment and acting as if she was actually that, she displays maternal behavior and in this way provides a new kind of support for him.

Finally, the reader finds Tuffy again in the fifth installment of *Dance*. Her responsibility here is, however, much different from anything prior. Rather than being affable and caring, she is a cold and unreceptive caretaker. With every movement she makes, Nick remarks on her forbidding character: "Her mysterious, equivocal presence [cast] a long, dark shadow over the scene" (180). Again, "Her smile cut like a knife" (181).

Her role has completely changed; thus she must carry this demeanor. Stringham's previous drinking habits, which were excessive, now require him to have a stern chaperone, one who can make sure that he stays sober and abides by doctor's orders. Trying to get him to leave a party early, especially one that he is the life of, would seem a difficult endeavor, but with relative ease, Tuffy demonstrates her authority over him by using her ingenuity. She convinces Stringham to accept a ride home by expertly pointing out that he cannot go anywhere else because he has forgotten his wallet, saying, "If I had only known ... I could have brought your notecase. It was lying on the table in your room" (184). Delivering the final blow, Tuffy finally forces Stringham to ride home with her. Here, acting as if she is a babysitter and it is the child's bedtime, she supports Stringham with tough love, which requires her to be firm and cold.

As Stringham ages, Tuffy Weedon becomes more involved in his life. Her personality has changed: progressing from a family friend to a praising mother, finally to a strict caretaker. Whether or not she will continue to care for Stringham is unclear, but I feel that he will still need some looking after in the future.

©John Bukawyn, 2008

THE DEPENDENT MACLINTICK
KATHERINE (LEONARD) CASCIO

If there were ever a need for a model of a dependent personality, Maclintick would be it. He exhibits "submissive and clinging behavior" and is unable to do "things on his ... own because of a lack of self esteem" (*DSM* 284) Maclintick's codependency escalates to the point where his wife becomes the dominant figure in their marriage; and although he attempts to fight back, he is still incapable of handling her wrath. However unhealthy their relationship becomes, in her he finds meaning; and when she leaves, he can no longer find reason to go on.

"Even the worst marriage [is] better than no marriage at all," (7) is the Strindbergian notion that Maclintick appears to live by. Even through his wife's relentless poking sarcasm and criticism, he returns to her for more, unable to leave her for fear of "being left alone to take care of himself" (*DSM*) 284). "Not surprising the poor woman had to go into a home after getting her divorce" (174), says Audrey candidly, speaking of a friend who had been married to a devotee of military marches, in the presence of her husband. She tells of "the sort of husband [she has] to put up with" (175). "Maclintick never dreams of going through the awful things he has done. It would take far too long." (176). She never ceases, never misses one opportunity to humiliate her husband. Yet, for every line she throws at him, he simply lets it hit him and goes on, seemingly unaffected by her condemnations. He "goes to excessive lengths" to receive attention from his wife, even "to the point of volunteering to [endure] things that are unpleasant" (*DSM* 284). Maclintick permits his wife's abusive behavior because he would rather be abused than be alone.

Obviously he is not innocent in his marriage; he dishes out his own fair share of insults throughout the book. From one-liners like "You bloody bitch" (151), to instances when others feel the tension between them, he does not appear completely devoid of confidence; he does fight back with his wife on occasion. "He swung around in such a rage that for a moment I though he was going to strike her"(151), Jenkins notes. Nonetheless, he never musters enough conviction to do more than rant and rave; he becomes complacent, even comfortable, in his despondent state. Maclintick has no one to blame but himself for his marital and dependency problems.

Contemporary psychiatrists would agree that Maclintick has Dependent Personality Disorder, in that he lacks the self-confidence required to become his own person. Hence, he must latch onto a comforting personality, whom he improbably finds in the form of Audrey. And when Audrey leaves him, he finds himself longing for the woman who gives him meaning. In the loss of his wife, his lifeline, Maclintick finds an adversity that he cannot overcome. Maclintick does not die when he gasses himself, but rather, he chooses to die when his wife leaves him.

Applying modern psychological theories to the historical and fictitious characters of *Dance to the Music of Time* only enhances how real they become. People encountered throughout *Casanova's Chinese Restaurant* may appear to be a stretch next to "normal" people. Still, knowing that Maclintick suffers from a true mental disorder verifies that the characters are not simply odd, made-up personalities, but rather, unique, dynamic, true-to-life people.

Source:

1. DSM-IV (Diagnostic and Statistical Manual of Mental Disorders). *American Psychiatric Associations' Diagnostic Criteria.* American Psychiatric Publishing, Inc. 2000.

CHAPTER 6:
THE KINDLY ONES

If I were to begin teaching – or reading, for that matter – *Dance* anywhere except with *A Question of Upbringing*, it would be with *The Kindly Ones*. It is a wonderful novel, dramatizing as it does the opening of two world wars. Dr. Trelawney's Sword of Mithras, "who each year immolates the sacred bull, will ere long now flash from its scabbard" (192). The book is wonderfully rich in mythological reference (obviously). It is structured with exceeding care, with balances everywhere – the wars, of course; the two framing characters of Trelawney and Uncle Giles; the look back at Nick's early days just halfway through the sequence; the death of Uncle Giles, who has guided Nick through the first six volumes and now sets him loose to find his own way through the last six.

I could have filled this book with just essays on *The Kindly Ones*, and they would all have been excellent. The students found a huge variety of subjects to write about: mythological references to war, appeasement and the Munich Accord, the Seven Deadly Sins, Alistair Crowley (model for Dr. Trelawney), Bracey's mental anguish, Billson's breakdown, Widmerpool's shift from abjection to power. And I have chosen four essays different from any of these!

All of the essays included here reflect the progression through *Dance*, each choosing an element from *The Kindly Ones* and looking back at its appearances in earlier volumes. This retrospection seems appropriate as we arrive at the halfway point of the series. Ash Verdery offers a moving description – a sort of obituary – of Uncle Giles. Zach Smotherman writes a second essay (the first having been written for *The Acceptance World*) about the influence of Nick's growing up as a military child. The first was good, but intuitive; this one has so much more material to work with, what with the Stonehurst section, that it arrives at an interesting conclusion about Nick's behavior. Jimmy Yang outlines an excellent analysis of Nick's bias against Bob Duport, which has always seemed to me to be a bit unfair, and as Jimmy gently suggests, a bit hypocritical, as well.

Finally, Nicole Lee gives us a fine piece comparing Nick Jenkins and Anthony Powell. The Stonehurst section provides her great material to work with. As I mentioned in the Introduction, the publication of her essay on the class website gave rise to a wonderful event. John Potter, who teaches at Kobe Yamate Women's Junior College in Japan, read the essays on-line and saw an article he had written listed as one of her sources. John wrote to the class about *The Kindly Ones* essays, and in it he thanked Nicole for citing his work.

We talked at length about John's letter – which I have included at the end of this chapter. Although my department spends several classes a year discussing plagiarism and the attribution of sources in writing, there's still a ho-hum attitude towards annotation. As far as the students are concerned, the only reason to bother with it is to avoid getting into trouble over literary dishonesty. But now, the fact that one of the sources had read their papers – in Japan! – and thanked Nicole for citing him, struck them forcibly. They understood that to write literary criticism – even for high school students – is to partake in the work of a global community; that, as we write, we are all having a kind of dialog with each other; and that each of our individual comments on a particular work can affect the understanding of everyone in the conversation. It was a transcendent moment.

Synopsis

The Kindly Ones begins at Stonehurst near Aldershot, in a flashback to Jenkins's childhood in 1914, with the house staff: Albert, the cook; Billson, the parlor maid; Bracey, the soldier-servant; and others. We learn of a domestic love-triangle. Billson loves Albert and Bracey loves Billson. Albert is not in love with anyone, but for some reason cannot resist the pressure of an unnamed "girl from Bristol," and gives notice to go marry her. On the day General and Mrs. Conyers are visiting, Billson, distraught, believing that she has seen a ghost, appears nude in the drawing room and gives her notice. General Conyers covers her up and calms her down. As the Conyers are leaving, Uncle Giles appears, carrying news of the outbreak of WWI.

In 1938 Jenkins and Isobel join Moreland and Matilda for a meal at Sir Magnus Donners' house. There they meet Templer and his new wife Betty. He now works for Donners. The dinner party turns into a photo-shoot re-creation of the Seven Deadly Sins. Widmerpool makes an appearance at the end of the chapter, condemning them for their unconventional behavior.

Jenkins learns of the death of Uncle Giles. He goes to the Bellevue, Albert's hotel, where Uncle Giles lived, to take care of funeral arrangements. There he runs into Bob Duport. They spend the evening together. Jenkins learns that Jean Duport has been more promiscuous than he knew. Jenkins and Duport free Dr. Trelawney -- also living at the Bellevue -- from the bathroom, where he is having an asthmatic attack. Eventually Ms. Erdleigh comes over to the Bellevue to give the doctor some "medicine."

Jenkins tries to have General Conyers expedite his entrance into the army, unsuccessfully. Conyers reveals he is marrying Tuffy Weedon. Jenkins then visits Widmerpool, already in the army, but receives no help there. The two men see Gypsy Jones giving a revolutionary speech outdoors; Widmerpool is greatly embarrassed. He asks Jenkins to help him get a lodger for his mother; they go to the Jeavons's house, where the lodger turns out to be the wife of Stanley Jeavons, Ted's brother. Stanley proves to be helpful in getting Jenkins called up from the list of reservists.

CHARACTER LIST

The major characters in this volume, arranged by chapter:

Chapter 1

Albert Creech – the Jenkinses' cook
Bracey – Capt. Jenkins's servant-soldier
Billson – the parlor maid
Edith – Jenkins's governess
Capt. Jenkins – Jenkins's father, stationed at Aldershot
Mrs. Jenkins –Jenkins's mother
General Conyers – friend of the Jenkinses
Bertha Conyers – wife of the general
Dr. Trelawney – a mystic, leader of a cult
Uncle Giles – Capt. Jenkins's brother

Chapter 2

Hugh Moreland – composer, Jenkins's best friend
Matilda – Moreland's wife
Isobel – Jenkins's wife
Peter Templer – businessman, old school friend of Jenkins
Betty – Templer's wife
Sir Magnus Donners – wealthy industrialist
Anne Stepney Umfraville – Donners's present mistress
Widmerpool – businessman, at school with Jenkins

Chapter 3

Bob Duport – Peter Templer's ex-brother-in-law
Mrs. Erdleigh – friend of Uncle Giles, fortune-teller

Chapter 4

Geraldine "Tuffy" Weedon – General Conyer's fiancée
Gypsy Jones – left-wing revolutionary

Lady Molly Jeavons – aunt of Isobel Jenkins
Ted Jeavons – Molly's husband
Mrs. Widmerpool – Widmerpool's terrifying mother
Stanley Jeavons – Ted's brother, an accountant

TRADITIONAL TO THE NOMAD
ASH VERDERY

Tetherless, Uncle Giles wanders through Anthony Powell's series *Dance to the Music of Time*, his visits, unexpected and often importunate, framing many of the books and accompanying Nick's development. He first appears in the series "through the narrow space released between the door and the wall" of Stringham's room at school (*QU* 14). In this scene he remains "cautious of assuming as a matter of course that his company would be welcome anywhere" (*QU* 15); his arrival prefigures the first adventure at school that Nick relates, when the housemaster, Le Bas, smells the smoke from Giles's "Turkish" cigarette. When Le Bas tells Nick that he must write to Giles to affirm that neither Stringham nor Nick smoked, Nick replies, "But I don't know his address, sir. All I know is that he was on his way to Reading" (*QU* 28). This unexpected and unwelcome arrival, and the subsequent adventure portray Giles's untethered existence. Nick summarizes this existence in a simple phrase regarding Giles's funeral; he says, "fire was the element appropriate to his obsequies, the funeral pyre traditional to the nomad" (147). Nick's comment epitomizes Giles; it metaphorically characterizes his wandering existence and defines him as an unsettled traveler.

His residences provide the major example of Giles's undomesticated nature, because they act more like "battered caravanserais," as he calls them, than permanent locations (141). Nick puts Giles in the "the proud, anonymous, secretive race that dwell in residential hotels" (149): two of these hotels are the Ufford in Bayswater, and the Bellevue in the unnamed "seaside town" (141). He describes both hotels as "battleship-grey... resolutely attempting to set out to sea" (149). This description demonstrates the transience of Giles's homes, because they, like him, seem ready to "ship anchor and float ... on the sluggish Bayswater tide" (149).

Giles's appearances – his unpredictable habit of popping up in random places at odd times – further exemplify his nomadic nature. His telegraphing Nick's parents asking, "Can you house me Sunday night?" is one example of these appearances, when he unexplainably arrived to "talk business" from Aldershot (46). This indefinite starting point and terminus portray the unattached quality of his nature. Throughout the novel Giles surfaces in random places; these wanderings demonstrate another aspect of his transient existence.

Giles's last effects, his bag left at the Bellevue, embody the third example of the propriety of Nick's nomad metaphor. Because, symbolically, all of his possessions can be contained in a Gladstone bag, Giles could travel anywhere unencumbered. He has lived a life on the move, his "residue" contained in suitcases left in residential hotels (154).

Nick's comment applies to Giles, because, like a nomad, he lacked a home, could travel unencumbered, and constantly wandered. Giles's life was filled with random acquaintances such as Trelawney and Mrs. Erdleigh, and unexplained locations such as Reading and Aldershot. He rambled in and out of Nick's life in pursuit of financial success. In the end, cremation really "was the element appropriate to his obsequies," because he truly was a nomad.

©Ashton Verdery, 2002

BEARING ARMOR FROM YOUTH
ZACHARY SMOTHERMAN

In *The Kindly Ones*, the military atmosphere under which Jenkins matures as a young boy has shaped his personality and more reserved nature. His character is influenced through his observation of his father, a military officer, his father's assistant, Private Bracey, and his family's friend, General Conyers. The Jenkins household, Stonehurst, is ruled by his father, a captain in the army, who, "had an absolute passion for power.... In his own house, only he himself was allowed to criticize"(38). The military lifestyle at home is a highly structured environment with high standards for behavior and conduct. In the first chapter, young Nicholas Jenkins embraces the military world of the adults around him and acts as if he is a soldier himself.

His father "was never greatly at ease with other men, ... avoiding friendship, too close personal ties which can handicap freedom of ascent"(38). This suggests that Jenkins is not exposed to many close adult male relationships as he grows up, but rather those of a more formal military style; and therefore he has little basis to form his own close friendships as he matures.

Jenkins is invited to a football match by Bracey, his father's soldier-servant. He is very excited to go because he will be able to observe military life more closely. Bracey has dressed up in his uniform for the excursion, which further intrigues young Jenkins. He says, "I was greatly interested in football but more on account of the closer contact the jaunt offered with military life"(23). The Jenkinses' home is secluded from daily military proceedings, because it is on a hill away from the base where the soldiers are stationed, so Jenkins does not get as much exposure to this world as he craves. When he asks his father if he can attend the football match, he says, "Permission was asked for the projected excursion. It was accorded by authority"(23). His language is very formal, as if he is an officer asking permission for a brief leave of duty. With this remark he demonstrates that he enthusiastically accepts the military world, seizing this opportunity to exercise the formalities of military life. This interaction also reveals the formal nature of his relationship with his father, his first male one in life.

Jenkins runs out the gate very excitedly to greet the Conyers as they arrive at Stonehurst to visit his family. As they approach, he comments on the General's old-fashioned goggles and hat, saying that they "seemed assumed, to some extent, ritualistically" (150), perhaps suggesting the mannerisms of the army. General Conyers questions Jenkins as to whether or not he attends school. Jenkins responds, "Not yet. I have lessons with Miss Orchard"(51). He goes on to name each child Miss Orchard teaches and his or her father's position in the army. General Conyers replies, "An exceedingly well informed report. You have given yourself a trouble to go into matters thoroughly, I see. That is one of the secrets of success in life" (51). This interaction gives Jenkins great pleasure; General Conyers is treating him as an adult in their conversation. Jenkins is truly able to fulfill the role of a soldier reporting to a higher officer. In fact, Jenkins has followed this code of conduct for the entire novel thus far, analyzing and observing every situation down to the finest detail before acting.

Through the observations of the military men around Jenkins, as he grows up at Stonehurst and as a result of his desire to imitate them and act like an adult soldier at a young age, he develops an emotionally reserved character and has few very close personal friends. He learns to love the structure of military life from his early childhood and tries to cling to it as he proceeds through his adult life. The rigid, military style and standards for friendship and behavior that he learns at Stonehurst affect his ability to interact socially. The upper class society that he pursues as a young adult creates a world of less certainty, and it is less clearly defined in terms of expectations compared to his more rigidly delineated military background. In consequence, he finds more emotionally distant relationships safer than the vulnerability that he might experience in more intimate ones.

COLORED VISION: NICK'S BIAS TOWARDS DUPORT
JIMMY YANG

We would like to think that Nick Jenkins is a trustworthy narrator. Throughout *A Dance to the Music of Time*, his relative detachment from the events he relates seems to indicate that he is unbiased toward the other characters in the story. He even seems to willingly omit information about characters that he cannot tell us about in an unbiased fashion, such as his wife and parents. In *The Kindly Ones*, however, we notice one character that Nick seems to dislike too unreasonably for him to provide an unbiased opinion. In the third chapter, Nick meets Bob Duport again for the first time since the first book in the series.

Back when we first met Duport, it was clear that Nick did not like him very much, since he was also after Jean. In most other respects, however, he seems similar to Nick's friend Peter Templer. Even Nick himself makes note of this similarity. "[Duport] had that indefinable air of being up to no good that characterized Peter himself" (*QU* 191). It seems reasonable therefore, that, since Nick is no longer in love with Jean, his impression of Bob might improve. However, when they meet again at the Bellevue, we find that this is not the case. Nick seems to hate him as much as ever.

From the beginning, we have seen the similarities between Duport and Templer. Both are stockbrokers who are interested in material things like "fast sports car, loud checks, blondes, golf, all that sort of thing" (99). While Templer complains about the state of Duport's marital affairs, Templer's own marriages have not fared much better than Duport's. Though Templer's marriage might not have been plagued by affairs, Duport's marriage lasted much longer than Templer's before a divorce.

Upon seeing Duport again in the Bellevue, Nick comments that he did "not like the way Duport behaved" (163-4). This seems odd, since much of his behavior is quite similar to what we have seen from Peter Templer in the past. Both of them show very little interest in Nick's writing career, or anything else highbrow. They also, unlike Nick, seem to have a rather skeptical view of the spiritual. Templer treats the Planchette board as sort of a joke, and Duport seems to take quite lightly Dr. Trelawney's talk of "the sword of Mithras ... flash[ing] from its scabbard" (192). All in all, there seems very little that might offend Nick in Duport's behavior that is not part of Templer's behavior as well.

Nick's history with Duport is undoubtedly one reason that his vision is so colored. He even says himself that "although I loved [Jean] no longer, our relationship had secreted this distasteful residue, an unalterable, if hidden, tie with her ex-husband" (163). Still, Duport may not deserve the loathing that he receives from Nick. He did not take Jean away from Nick, but in some ways, it was the other way around. At the very least he might be entitled to some sympathy from Nick, especially when the conversation turns to her many affairs. When Nick finds out about her affair with Brent, he can only focus on his own surprise. "I felt as if someone had suddenly kicked my legs out from under me, so that I had landed on the other side of the room, not exactly hurt, but thoroughly ruffled, with all the breath knocked out of me" (178). His only feeling remotely resembling sympathy is his momentary urge to tell Duport about his own affair, but other thoughts quickly silence that.

There is another possibility for the difference between Nick's views of Peter and of Bob. Perhaps it is not that Nick dislikes Duport much more than he ought, but that he likes Templer more than he should. They have a shared history, a friendship (or what remains of one) that has built up over many years. Even when he first knew Templer at school, Nick was unsure about whether he liked him, since his "boast that he had never read a book for pleasure in his life did not predispose me in his favor" (*QU* 8). Nick was with him for the Old Boy dinner, and introduced him to J.G. Quiggin, whom Templer's first wife, Mona, would leave him for. Nick has watched the ups and downs in Templer's life, and perhaps his sympathy for him comes from years of acquaintance, which cannot be substituted, in Duport's case, with an hour or so in a bar.

Perhaps it is in Nick's nature to hold a grudge. It seems just as well that if our narrator's memories last as long as they do, his grudges, or his sympathies, might last for a long time as well. Just as Nick's past affair with Jean sours his relationship with Duport, so do his memories with Templer improve Nick's impression of him. One thing is for certain: though he may seem reliable on many occasions, we see from his opinion of Bob Duport that Nick is not always a perfect narrator, and perhaps in the future, we may need to take some of his opinions with a grain of salt.

©James Yang, 2008

POWELL'S LIFE: NICK JENKINS AND HIS AUTHOR
NICOLE LEE

As we have come across many character models in *A Dance to the Music of Time*, such as Constant Lambert for Hugh Moreland and George Orwell for Lord Warminster, it can only be assumed that Anthony Powell himself is a model for the narrator, Nick Jenkins. This becomes especially clear in *The Kindly Ones*, as Powell finally reveals Nick's childhood through flashbacks and details about his parents. Many aspects of Powell's early life prove to be reflected in some of Nick's experiences as a child.

First off, Powell's parents bear striking resemblances to Nick's in their mannerisms and way of life. Powell's mother "above all things detested having attention drawn to herself, even in a complimentary manner" (*Infants* 39). Likewise, Nick's mother does not enjoy "going out" and has a great distaste for officers' wives, or "regimental" ladies (22). She stays to herself and seems rather reserved, from what we know of her in the novel. Mrs. Powell and Mrs. Jenkins also both share a common belief in occultism. Powell's mother always showed a slight interest in divination as he stated in his memoirs, "My mother possessed none of her sister's (and mother-in-law's) fortune-telling flair, although in her younger days she too had not been at all adverse to the Occult and its byways… She also retained a life-long interest in Christian Science" (*Infants* 39). Similarly, in *The Kindly Ones*, Jenkins describes, "My mother – together with her sisters in their unmarried days – had always indulged a taste for investigation of the Unseen World" (5). Powell's grandmother was also much devoted to such pursuits as occultism and fortune-telling. All of this exposure to the Occult as a child offers a possible explanation of all the references to divination in *A Dance to the Music of Time*, particularly in *The Acceptance World* when the characters play Planchette and Mrs. Erdleigh brings out her fortune-telling cards.

Just as Powell's mother resembles Nick's, his father can be related to the character of Captain Jenkins. For six years during his early childhood, Powell's father was posted to the Kensington Regiment, a London battalion of the Territorial Army. During this time, their family lived in a flat in Kensington. In 1913 his father rejoined the regiment at Aldershot, and the family moved to Stonehurst. In the novel, Jenkins' father is also involved in the war and stationed at Aldershot. Inevitably, a job in the military comes with a military lifestyle, which both Powell's and Jenkins' parents successfully follow. Anthony Powell sums this up in his memoirs, writing: "My parents' marriage was a wholehearted success" (*Infants* 38).

In *Dance*, before marriage, Nick's mom was "keen enough on parties and balls, but, my father having little or no taste for such amusements, she forgot about them herself, then developed greater dislike than his own" (22). However, Nick's father does have a character flaw that "Happy marriage did not cure" (37). The idea for this flaw probably originated from the Captain Powell's personality; he is said to have possessed an "untranquil temperament," having rows and showing himself difficult at many times (*Infants* 38). Nick's father apparently shares this characteristic as he mentions in the novel, "My father would sometimes rebel against this aggressive, even contagious, depression- to which he himself was no stranger- and then there would be a row. (12)" He feels that "all tragedies are major tragedies ... especially if he himself is in any way concerned" (27). It is clear that Powell used many observations of his own parents to create Captain and Mrs. Jenkins.

Just as the characters in *Dance* are modeled on Powell's actual life, the places are as well. In particular, Stonehurst is not an imaginary place, but rather a large, furnished bungalow where Powell spent many of his childhood years. He also notes memories of the appearances of a cult leader who ran past the gates from time to time with his followers, similar to Dr. Trelawney (*Infants* 54). Powell even states, "We lived in a large bungalow of Indian type, let furnished, its situation on the top of a lonely hill, surrounded by heather, gorse, pines, sandy hollows skirted with bracken... A fairly close description of the bungalow ... appears in my novel ... in which the house is called Stonehurst" (*Infants* 51).

One last parallel that can be drawn from Powell's life to the occurrences in the novel is the ghost incident. In his memoirs, Powell tells how his own mother encountered ghosts at Stonehurst. Their family owned many animals, some of which slept on her bed. He explains, "One night, my mother awakened by the thud of a smallish animal jumping on her bed ... The thing landed near the foot of the bed and slowly worked its way up, until pressing down the bedclothes just below her neck. This visitation took place several times" (*Infants* 55). When we begin *The Kindly Ones*, we learn of the ghosts immediately, as they are "a recognized feature of Stonehurst" (4). "My mother admitted to a recurrent sense, sometimes even in the day, of an uncomfortable presence in her bedroom ...; at night, she had waked once or twice overwhelmed with an inexplicable feeling of doom and horror" (4). As talk of ghosts was not curtailed in Nick's childhood, it is not surprising to find these references in *The Kindly Ones*.

Anthony Powell uses much of his own life as a model for the plot in *A Dance To the Music of Time*. The details of Powell's life are, as might be expected, very substantially the same as Nick Jenkins's. An examination of Powell's memoirs reveals that much of the narrator's childhood is in fact drawn from Powell's life.

Sources:

1. Allen, Brooke. "The Unauthorized Anthony Powell." http://newcriterion.com:81/archive/23/sept04/powell.htm. 24 Jan. 2008
2. Potter John. "The Novelist and His Narrator: Anthony Powell and Nicholas Jenkins." June 1999. *Anthony Powell Resources Pages*. http://www.anthonypowell.org.uk. 24 Jan. 2008
http://www.anthonypowell.org.uk/reflib/narrator.pdf 24 Jan. 2008

3. Powell, Anthony. *Infants of the Spring.* Heinemann. London, 1976.

A Letter from John Potter
Kobe Yamate Women's Junior College, Japan

Once again many thanks to you and your students for the essays on *The Kindly Ones*, which I've read as always with great interest. No time to go into any great detail but I was especially interested in these ones because *The Kindly Ones* is rather a favourite of mine and I think the first chapter is a little self-contained gem. So I was pleased to see Billson and Bracey given some attention by Alex Svec and others. Another of my favourite characters (I don't really know why) is Uncle Giles and so I very much enjoyed Corey Simpson's farewell to him and the intimate tone of her essay. Yes, Giles is infuriating at times, but his death does come as an unpleasant shock as we have grown so used to his grumbling ways. Nick Anschuetz's essay links very cleverly the appeasement of Germany and Uncle Giles' own appeasement and I especially liked the way he did this, as he made me think of it in a rather startling new way. Alyssa too describes the Munich agreement very well, and so I have been able to brush up on my history a bit as well.

Oh, and I mustn't forget to say thank you to that wise young woman Nicole Lee who has quoted an article of mine as a source for her paper on the parallels between Jenkins and Powell. Thanks for reading it, Nicole! And thanks to everyone for these excellent essays as you have now reached half way in the series.

I hope you are all well. Snowflakes have begun to fall outside my window here in Mie, Japan as I write this, reminding me of the start of the *Dance*.

CHAPTER 7:
THE VALLEY OF BONES

With *The Valley of Bones* we began the war trilogy of *Dance*. I was worried – both years, actually – about whether this section would hold their interest, but I had a few World War II history buffs that found Nick's unusual perspective of this conflict bracing. They had never considered what the war was like for those not in combat, and were interested in what transpired on the island world of Britain while combat raged across the Channel. And those not interested in blood and glory were drawn in by the characters of Bithel and Gwatkin.

One of the stylistic mannerisms – and, yes, annoyances – of the war trilogy is the military's love of alphabet soup. There are countless acronyms for ranks, for places, for branches of service; and Powell does not miss an opportunity to insert any one of them. Will Story, bless him, wrote a dictionary of all these abbreviations. For those who are now reading *The Valley of Bones* and using this book as a companion, I can offer you the solace of looking ahead to Chapter 9 and finding Will's invaluable aid, titled "Learning the ABC of Military Affairs."

In this chapter, Gauri Kirloskar reacted with uncommon prescience to the sudden, malevolent appearance of Widmerpool. She predicts the plot of *The Soldier's Art* almost perfectly, with Widmerpool's ill-fated machinations with Hogbourne-Johnson and Sunny Farebrother. Nick Anschuetz produced a clear and perceptive comparison between the bones in the passage from Ezekiel and the raising of the British army for World War II. And Erica Bakies found herself doing family history. Her grandfather grew up in Ireland during the war, and she was able to interview him to learn from a first-hand source what the conditions were like for Nick Jenkins when he served in Northern Ireland. It was exciting for all of us to find suddenly such a close connection to the unfamiliar material of the novel.

The final essay here reprises Katherine Cascio's interest in psychology, building on the piece she wrote on Maclintick in the *Casanova's Chinese Restaurant* chapter. It thus demonstrates one useful application for our internet publication, by allowing a student to develop further an idea from an earlier paper, and actually make reference to that work in a meaningful way.

Synopsis

The Valley of Bones begins in Wales in early 1940. Jenkins arrives at the Anti-Gas Warfare School, where he first must deal with the poor bed-making skills of his new platoon. Together with a number of the junior officers, he helps make a dummy and lays it in Bithel's bed as a "rag." Bithel, who is drunk, acts as if the dummy is a woman, embarrassing everyone. Jenkins learns that Bithel's reputation as a relative of a Victory Cross winner and a famous rugby player is false.

The company is sent to Castlemallock, in Northern Ireland. Deafy Morgan is attacked and his rifle stolen, the event being blamed on Bithel. During a field exercise, Gwatkin messes up royally by having his company fall far behind schedule. Sgt. Pendry, who learns his wife is having an affair back home, dies ambiguously, either from an attack or from suicide.

Jenkins encounters Pennistone and Barnby on his way to a course at Aldershot. There he meets Odo Stevens, a free-spirited officer, and runs into Jimmy Brent, who tells him he had an affair with Jean Duport. Afterwards, Jenkins spends a leave at Frederica's. There he learns Flavia Wisebite is involved with Robert and Dicky Umfraville is engaged to Frederica. Odo Stevens, who drives Jenkins there, makes a hit with Pricilla. Buster Foxe shows up in great distress; Mrs. Foxe is divorcing him. As Jenkins and Stevens leave, Isobel announces she is about to have their baby.

Back at Castlemallock, Gwatkin introduces Jenkins to the object of his infatuation, the barmaid Maureen. Later, Bithel, drunk, apparently tries to kiss the bartender at the officer's mess. Gwatkin arrests him, but forgets to file the report the next day. Then he forgets to pass on proper codes to Jenkins and the other officers. The upshot of all this is that Bithel is promoted to the head of the Mobile Laundry, and Gwatkin is relieved of his command. Jenkins is reassigned to the office of the DAAG (Deputy Assistant Adjutant General). On a farewell walk, Gwatkin and Jenkins discover Maureen in an embrace with Gwylt. Jenkins reports to the DAAG, to discover – with dismay – that it is Widmerpool.

CHARACTER LIST

The major characters in this volume, arranged by chapter:

Chapter 1

2nd Lieut. Idwal Kedward – a platoon commander
CSM Cadwallander – the Company Sergeant-Major
Capt. Roland Gwatkin – Company Commander
Sgt. Pendry – Jenkins's platoon sergeant
Lt. Yanto Breeze – a platoon commander
Lt. Bithel – older, a newly arrived commissioned officer

Chapter 2

Cpl. Gwylt – cheerfully womanizing NCO
Lance Cpl. Gittins – CSM Cadwallander's brother-in-law
Pvt. Sayce – the company bad character
Pvt. Deafy Morgan – a good soldier, hard of hearing
General Liddament – imperious general, Commander of Division

Chapter 3

David Pennistone – officer, met years ago at Milly Andriadis's party
Odo Stevens – officer met at course at Aldershot
Jimmy Brent – old friend of Peter Templer
Pricilla Budd – Nick's sister-in-law
Pricilla Lovell – ditto
Robert Tolland – Nick's brother-in-law
Flavia Wisebite – Stringham's sister, enamored of Robert
Isobel – Nick's wife
Dicky Umfraville – former nightclub manager, engaged to Frederica
Buster Foxe – Stringham's stepfather

Chapter 4

Maureen – an Irish barmaid, Gwatkin's Irish infatuation
Widmerpool – himself

Why Bones?
Nicholas Anschuetz

Every installment of Anthony Powell's *Dance to the Music of Time* series has a title that either metaphorically or literally relates to the story of that specific novel. For example, the first book is titled *A Question of Upbringing* because it tells the story of the preparatory school days of Nick, Stringham, Templer, and Widmerpool and highlights the characters' differences. Less figuratively, the fourth book is called *At Lady Molly's* because Nick meets his future wife and learns of Widmerpool's upcoming marriage at Lady Molly's house. Nevertheless, no title in the series we have read so far is as poignant or mystical as the seventh installment's, *The Valley of Bones*. At a glance, the title seems a complete non-sequitor. However, the title not only explains what's in the novel, but also helps our understanding of it as well.

The phrase "valley of bones" comes from Ezekiel 37, the text of the sermon that Popkiss preaches to the soldiers at the end of Chapter One. In the passage, God leads Ezekiel to a valley filled with the bones of dead Israelites. God then instructs Ezekiel to prophesy the word of the Lord to the bones, and the bones begin to stand upright and become human again. The resurrected then become Ezekiel's army to reclaim Israel. The overarching story of Powell's *The Valley of Bones* almost directly parallels this narrative in numerous ways.

The first mention of bones in the novel comes on page 2:

> Although [Nick's ancestors] had remained in these parts only a couple of generations, there was an aptness, something fairly inexorable, in reporting under the badges of second-lieutenant to a spot from which quite a handful of forerunners of the same blood had set out to become unnoticed officers of Marines or the East India Company; as often as not

to lay twenty-year-old bones in the cemeteries of
Bombay and Mysore.

He remarks that he is training to become a second lieutenant in
Wales at the same place where his ancestors had trained to become
officers many years before. The phrase "to lay twenty-year-old
bones in the cemeteries of Bombay and Mysore" establishes a
connection between the two generations. Nick is simply the
reincarnation of his ancestors, a symbol of their bones rising up
to fight again.

The "valley of bones" also refers to the British Army after the
First World War. Out of 2.6 million enlisted men, over 1.6 million
were wounded and over 650,000 were confirmed killed. ("British
Army") Britain spent the years in between the two world wars
rebuilding their infrastructure rather than their military. When
World War Two broke out, Britain had initially to scramble to
survive. They had at their disposal seemingly only a valley of dry
bones with which to make an army.

The soldiers with whom Nick has interactions are truly made
from random bones scattered across a valley floor. None of them
are fighters: Nick is a writer, and most of the others are miners or
engaged in some other nonviolent profession. Most of them are
not very good at what they do; Bithel is an alcoholic, Nick is too
old for his rank and is found not to be a good field commander,
Gwylt is a womanizer, Deafy Morgan is practically deaf, Sayce
is Gomer Pyle gone bad, General Liddament is dictatorial, and
Captain Gwatkin is such a bad company commander that he is
relieved of his duties due to incompetence. The army is so ragtag
that even Widmerpool, the most unlikely of all the characters,
makes major.

Another correlation between *The Valley of Bones* and Ezekiel 37
is that in each story the "bones" all come from a single particular
place. In Ezekiel 37, the bones all come from Israel. In the novel,
they all come from Wales. Powell emphasizes this sense of place by
calling attention to Nick's incongruity. Instead of English names
like Stringham, Templer, and Tolland, the reader sees almost

alien names, like Gwatkin, Cadwallander, and Idwal Kedward. This makes the reader recognize immediately he is not in familiar territory, while at the same time creating a sense of unity among the Welsh characters. In chapter two, the soldiers sing "Cwm Rhondda," a popular Welsh hymn as they leave their homes as if to carry their Welsh heritage with them. "The men, although departing from their own neighbourhoods and country, were in a fairly buoyant mood. Something was beginning at last. They sang softly...." (39). These soldiers are proud to be Welshmen just as the Ezekiel's soldiers are proud to be Israelites.

By creating this world parallel to Ezekiel 37, Powell creates an ethereal and otherworldly aura around war in general. War is certainly not something that touches most of us in a direct way. To those it does touch, it is something completely apart from normal life. Powell's allegory beautifully draws attention to this distinction.

Source:

1. "British Army in the First World War." *Sparticus Educational.* http://www.spartacus.schoolnet.co.uk/FWWbritain.htm. 14 Feb 2008.

©Nicholas Anschuetz, 2008

Almost at the Top
Gauri Kirloskar

In *The Valley of Bones*, the evolution of Widmerpool's character bursts on us like an explosion as he moves to a higher and more powerful position. Even though he does not appear until the last few pages of the book, his sudden presence is dominating; Jenkins says, "he was undeniably a somewhat formidable figure" (240) as the DAAG. This is the first time Jenkins has directly called Widmerpool a threat; he is not only powerful, but he now, for the first time, has power over Jenkins' himself.

A DAAG is a Deputy Assistant Adjutant General, a highly esteemed job usually reserved for trustworthy efficient young officers or to older ones who will not move up to the rank of Lt. Colonel for reasons of fitness, age, etc. Widmerpool has obtained this position as a result of hard work, and Jenkins is now under his command. However, will Widmerpool's greed for power entice him to try to take over positions of his senior officials?

Along with his rise in power, Widmerpool's level of confidence and self-esteem have also reached new heights. "So long as I remain, the work will be properly done" (241). He believes in his ability to do good work, thereby ensuring his place high up on the power ladder. "I make sure [Col. Hogbourne-Johnson] can find nothing to complain of in my work" (241). He protects his job stability by making sure there is nothing he can be fired for, and he is in total control of his military position. He is as meticulous as ever, as can be seen from the detail in his dictation over the phone. He puts in his best effort, which is admirable, but his haughtiness soon shows through in his conversation with Jenkins.

"Now I thrive on work, but I saw at once that even I must have assistance" (241), he says. Widmerpool is, as always, self-centered, full of himself. His conceit is portrayed clearly through his priggish comments. His remarks to Jenkins are condescending. "I take it you did not find yourself specially cut out to be a regimental officer" (242), "Let's hope you will be better adapted to other duties" (242). He mocks Jenkins' abilities as a soldier. In fact, in *The Kindly Ones* Jenkins asks Widmerpool to pull him into the army, but Widmerpool refuses. He wants to be at the top of the military rat race, and has absolutely no interest in helping others along the way.

We have seen Widmerpool in this superior position before – except he was over Duport, not Jenkins. Now he is in a position of power, but it is doubtful that he will ever be satisfied. He can only expected to reach further; he might try to outmaneuver his senior officers and this might get him in hot water. On the other hand, he might even get on top of the situation the same way he did with Duport - by altering the situation in his favor and hanging his subordinate out to dry. Jenkins will be directly affected by Widmerpool's tactics to get to his desired level of supremacy, now that he is under Widmerpool's command.

WORLD WAR II:
NICK'S ADVENTURE ON THE EMERALD ISLE
ERICA BAKIES

World War II was a time when Ireland was just beginning to create an identity for itself as a new country, separate from England. In *The Valley of Bones*, Nick describes border attacks and hears about Maureen's experience as an Irish citizen. The historical context in which his tour of duty is performed is a crucial one to Ireland's past. Right before WWII, the country was torn into two major regions. Northern Ireland, around 90% Protestant, wanted independence from Ireland ("Reform"). Nick's troops in *The Valley of Bones* were there to protect the Northern Irish from the war, and also to try to create some peace on the border during such a difficult time in Ireland's history.

During WWII, Ireland declared neutrality on all fronts as a small, newly formed country. The country itself did not feel comfortable entering a conflict that may have ended up creating more hardships, as they were already cast in a shadow of controversy. On the other hand, Northern Ireland allied with the British forces. The Nationalists were people who favored the country staying together as one. Those that lived in Northern Ireland cried out with anguish at having to live in a country that had temporarily given power to the British. However, even Eamon DeValera, Ireland's newly appointed prime minister, had sympathetic urges towards the British. He often allowed those Allied soldiers who parachuted into Ireland to "accidentally" escape to British-controlled Northern Ireland ("Reform").

Nick's experiences in the novel pertain specifically to the disruptions on the border between Northern Ireland and Ireland. According to my grandfather, who was only 13 years old at the time living in Kilarney, Ireland, border raids were frequent. Just as a few years ago, when IRA bombings occurred on the boundary and fights showed up every other day in the newspapers, in 1940 the border where Nick was stationed was constantly under attack. It wasn't uncommon for people to cross the border, vandalize, and then return to their own side. The British army was there to make sure that things stayed under control, as well as protect the Irish citizens in case WWII broke out in Ireland. Robbing the soldiers stationed there became a regular occurrence, just as when Deafy Morgan was attacked and his rifle stolen.

My grandfather also told me about how upset the Nationalists were in Northern Ireland. In Northern Ireland, if you didn't own a house you couldn't vote. With the limited number of jobs available, it wasn't surprising that people didn't own homes. Over 14,000 Irish citizens left to work in Britain at the outbreak of war ("Side"). The Nationalists, who wanted Ireland to remain as a whole country, often claimed they couldn't express their feelings in the democratic system because they couldn't vote. They were often harassed and hurt by the (usually Protestant) land-owning citizens of Northern Ireland. This became another source of conflict that the British forces were there to deal with, and could have led to the situation Maureen was in. Her family crossed the border to be in Northern Ireland under the protection of the British troops, but she was clearly a Nationalist.

When the war broke out, over 70,000 volunteers left Ireland to fight in the British army ("Side"). At the end of our conversation, my grandfather began to recall old friends who died in the war. "They would have been around 90 or 100 now ... if they had survived," he said. As a little boy living in the country, my grandfather never heard much about the war. His family didn't own a radio, and the newspaper came maybe once a week from someone who went to town. News of the war affected the Irish families, and the British army, like Nick's, was there to support the government in a desperate time of war and civil conflict. As my grandfather said, "An awful lot of Irish boys gave their lives in World War II."

Sources:

1. "The Reform Movement." http://www.reform.org/TheReformMovement_files/article_files/articles/war.htm. 12 Feb. 2008
2. "On Which Side Did Ireland Fight?" http://wiki.answers.com/Q/On_which_side_did_Ireland_fight_during_World_War_2. 13 Feb 2008

UMFRAVILLE'S FIVE
KATHERINE (LEONARD) CASCIO

Dicky Umfraville is a rather zany character with enormous misfortune when it comes to matters of the heart. In *The Valley of Bones*, he himself admits, "I don't have much luck with wives" (156). He has married four times, and is now going for number five by marrying Frederica. His wives have either left him for other men or died shortly after the wedding. All in all, Umfraville never seems able to hold on to love. This is probably why he so desperately wants to try again with Frederica, whom he believes will "be my salvation" (156). But why does Umfraville believe that simply getting married again will solve his problems? Four marriages have already failed, so what keeps driving him to keep on proposing?

His first wife was Dolly, an "absolute stunner" (152). He tells Jenkins that at first she did not want to marry him. "Asked her again and again. The answer was always no. Then one day she changed her mind, the way women do" (152). He recalls that his "pertinacity" won her over; however, it never appeared that Dolly was in love with him, at least not in the way he loved her. It was always "'Not tonight, darling, because I don't love you enough', then 'Not tonight, darling, because I love you too much'" (153). Eventually, Dolly left him for Buster Foxe, pleading for a divorce. His first marriage ended within two years.

Umfraville's next wife was Joy Grant, a woman whom he describes as somewhat of a prostitute. He tells Jenkins that she was a "very suitable one too – so I thought I might as well marry her" (155). Soon after they wed, they left for Kenya, where they realized that they had "made a mistake in becoming man and wife" (155). Joy deserted him for a man named Castlemallock. When Castlemallock proved unsuitable, she left him for a jockey named Jo Breen. Umfraville's second marriage ended just after it began.

Umfraville realized that "the business of wives departing was...becoming a positive habit" (156); yet, he took up with the wife of the District Commissioner, a marriage doomed before it started: "she died of enteric six months" (156) after they wed.

Next, he tried to marry Lady Anne Stepney, which "was a crazy thing to do"(156), attributed partly to the vast age difference between the two. This marriage, needless to say, "didn't last long" (156). Umfraville will marry Frederica next and he claims they will be "the model married couple" (156). However, after his track record of four previous failures, how can he be so sure?

It seems that Umfraville may suffer from a variation of what Maclintick suffers from, a case of dependence upon others. Obviously their types of dependency differ. Maclintick is a pathetic, hopeless character; a repellant man that only holds onto his wife because he stands no chance of attaining another woman. Umfraville, on the other hand, is charming and attractive; he can and does succeed with the opposite sex. Still, although both men are vastly different, neither can seem to live without a woman by his side. Maclintick sticks with one wretch of a woman for many years, while Umfraville jumps from wife to wife.

One of the defining characteristics of Dependent Personality Disorder that Umfraville exhibits is that he "urgently seeks another relationship...when a close relationship ends" (*DSM* 284). Maclintick, on the other hand, shows characteristics "submissive and clinging behavior" and "has difficulty...[in] doing things on his own because of a lack of self-esteem"(*DSM* 284). Both men have the same Dependent Personality Disorder; it simply manifests itself in drastically different ways.

Source:

1. DSM-IV (Diagnostic and Statistical Manual of Mental Disorders). *American Psychiatric Associations' Diagnostic Criteria*. American Psychiatric Publishing, Inc. 2000.

©Katherine (Leonard) Cascio, 2002

CHAPTER 8:
THE SOLDIER'S ART

I find *The Soldier's Art* one of the more difficult novels in the sequence to teach. True, there are formal elements that can keep us going. It's written in the form of a sonata – A-B-A – and the students can understand and appreciate that, can follow the narrative as it moves from Division to London and back to Division and Widmerpool. In fact, all the essays I have chosen for this chapter are formal literary analyses: the uses of silence and noise, the metaphor of theater, the close reading of Browning's lines from *Childe Roland to the Dark Tower Came*, and a very perceptive essay suggesting that the rhythm of war – with its hurry-up-and-wait nature – provides the structure for the novel.

This last piece suggests why *The Soldier's Art* is difficult to teach, at least for high schoolers – and, I suspect, for undergraduates. Not very much happens. Much of *Dance* takes time to develop, so the students aren't surprised, but there's no startling new character to meet – no Jean, no Moreland, no Dr. Trelawney, no Gwatkin, and Pamela Flitton and Scorpio Murtlock lie ahead. There's no startling event, either – no sugar poured on an angry Widmerpool, nor a Karl Marx writing to Quiggin with Planchette. The most memorable moments are deaths – Bijou Ardglass, Chips Lovell, Lady Molly, Pricilla. And Stringham is as good as dead, too. It's a sad book, overall, as we begin to lose some of the friends we've known for the past seven volumes.

As Alyssa Warren notes, the only other major plot concern is the trouble Widmerpool's intriguing might create for himself, but even that all but evaporates, despite Sunny Farebrother's machinations.

So it's no wonder that so many of the papers for this book fell into literary criticism, rather than into research or parody or personal reflection. In some ways *The Soldier's Art* offers more interior views of its characters than other books in *Dance*, and surely interior views invite analysis. We see deeper into

Stringham, into Max Pilgrim, even into Ted Jeavons than ever before. Naturally the students wrote about what they saw. Nick Anschuetz's essay – which I did not include in its entirety – suggests one other reason why this shift occurs:

> Although the story has become more depressing, it has also become much more interesting. In the beginning of the fall term, I felt no connection between the characters and myself. However, as the tale unfolded, I began to see that these characters were not just aristocrats, but rather people, who were stuck in an aristocratic position. Although their hardships are not those of the common man or soldier during this era, they still have a story to tell, and it is World War II that makes it worth hearing.

Nick is right, I think; the war has leveled this playing field. It has turned all of the characters towards a common cause, and class distinctions have eroded completely. Charles Stringham has become a mess waiter, after all, Widmerpool a major; and we need to look at the interior of each character to find out how and why these changes have occurred. A sort of democracy has been unleashed upon the Dancers.

SYNOPSIS

The Soldier's Art opens in 1941. The Division is still in Ireland. General Liddament takes an interest in Jenkins and arranges for him to see a Major Finn in London for a new post. During an exercise, Widmerpool is embarrassed by Hogbourne-Johnson, who chews him out unfairly for a mess-up with the traffic circuits. Stringham unexpectedly appears as a waiter in F Mess, where Biggs is mean to him. He and Jenkins chat privately, mentioning Robert Tolland's death.

On leave in London, Jenkins applies to Finn for a posting with the Free French, but his French is not good enough. Later he has a drink with Chips Lovell, who tells him Pricilla, his wife, is having an affair with Odo Stevens and then goes to the Madrid to find her at Bijou Ardglass's fortieth birthday party. After Chips leaves, he dines with Moreland and Mrs. Maclintick - now a couple! - and, by coincidence, Pricilla and Odo appear and join them. Pricilla becomes upset and leaves. After dinner, at the Morelands, Jenkins meets their lodger, Max Pilgrim, who tells him that Bijou and Chips, among others, were killed at the Madrid in a blitz. Jenkins goes to the Jeavons's to find Pricilla, and discovers that both she and Lady Molly have been killed as well, by a bomb from a different blitz.

Back at the DAAG's office, Widmerpool is leaving the Division, but will do nothing to help Jenkins find a new post. One night Stringham and Jenkins try to help Bithel, who is drunk, but Widmerpool discovers them. Widmerpool drums Bithel out of the army and gets Stringham reposted to the Mobile Laundry, knowing that he will be sent to the Far East, thus getting him out of his hair. He accuses Diplock, Hogbourne-Johnson's assistant, of embezzling, but the colonel defends his man. Widmerpool's maneuvering to appoint certain officers to important posts is discovered by the General, landing him in hot water. Diplock deserts to independent Ireland. As Widmerpool tries to deal with his troubles, Jenkins receives orders for a posting to London, not to the dreaded ITC.

CHARACTER LIST

The major characters in this volume, arranged by chapter:

Chapter 1

Widmerpool – himself
Lt. Bithel – recently appointed head of Mobile Laundry
General Liddament – Commander of Division
Col. Hogbourne Johnson – in charge of operational duties
Col. Pedlar – "A and Q" (quartermaster)
Capt. Biggs – Company Physical Training Officer
Pvt. Charles Stringham – Jenkins's old school friend, a mess waiter
(Mr. Diplock – Hogbourne-Johnson's chief clerk, never actually appears)

Chapter 2

Maj. Finn - liaison officer in charge of Free French
David Penniston - acquaintance of Jenkins, works for Finn
Chips Lovell - married to Pricilla Tolland, Jenkins's sister-in-law
Hugh Moreland - composer, Jenkins's good friend
Audrey Maclintick - living with Moreland
Odo Stevens - acquaintance of Jenkins, having affair with Pricilla
Max Pilgrim - entertainer, Moreland's lodger
Eleanor Walpole-Wilson - old friend of Jenkins

Chapter 3

Cheesman – new commander of Mobile Laundry
Sgt. Ablett – in Mobile Laundry

THE RHYTHM OF WAR AS A TEMPLATE FOR PLOT
ALYSSA WARREN

In *The Soldier's Art*, Nick Jenkins' account of the Second World War unfolds, following a rhythm of sudden blitzes and air raids. The plot forces us to feel as if we are in fact sitting in Britain during the mid-1940s. As it is difficult for his readers to grasp the idea of living in wartime, Powell writes with a pattern of long stretches of routine matter, daily life in the army, and other tedious anecdotes – interrupted with sudden bursts of action. Thus the style of this book offers us some insight into the cadence of military life.

The beginning of *The Soldier's Art* is notably unexciting. Nick buys an overcoat. Nick reminisces about his Moreland days. Nick comments on his daily life in the F Mess. Nick and Bithel converse about the books they read in their boyhoods. These commonplace accounts seem lackluster when one considers the intensity of war. Sixteen pages into the book, Bithel and Jenkins, along with the other men of the F Mess, experience an air raid. Bithel indicates that the raid is "more spectacular than alarming, even a trifle stimulating now one [is] fully awake and dressed; so long as the mind [does] not dwell on the tedium of a three-day exercise the following day, undertaken after a missed night's sleep" (16-7). This comment explicitly demonstrates the tedium of military exercises, on which much of the time in the army is spent.

The deaths of Chips Lovell, Priscilla Tolland, and Molly Jeavons occur suddenly and in quick succession. Max Pilgrim informs Nick, Moreland, and Audrey Maclintick that "no one survived from that corner" of the Madrid where Bijou Ardglass' party was seated. At this table was Chips Lovell. This news shocks Nick, as he had just conversed with Chips hours prior to the blitz that hit the Madrid. Nick, Moreland, and Audrey react to this tragic event for mere minutes until Audrey states, "I'll make some tea" (158). Audrey quickly returns to her normal routine by putting a pot of tea on the stove to end a social night. As Audrey makes the tea, Nick realizes that "Priscilla [has] to be told about the Madrid as soon as possible" (158). Without grieving, Nick returns to his matter-of-fact nature and leaves Moreland's flat to bring the news to the Jeavons.

Upon arriving at the Jeavonses' house a few hours later, Nick is informed that their house has been hit during the most recent air raid and that Molly Jeavons has been killed. Nick enters the house to speak with Eleanor Walpole-Wilson, who adds that Priscilla has also been killed in the blast. Eleanor begins to cry, "It's all too awful" (164). Moments later, she says, "We must get out some sort of plan. No good just sitting about" (164). Again, the characters quickly return to normal life after tragic interruptions.

These dramatic events resulting in the deaths of three prominent characters fall upon Nick and us suddenly and forcefully in a manner similar to that of an air raid. Furthermore, they end the way air raids end:

> Now noise was diminishing, the barrage gradually, though appreciably, reducing in volume. Quite suddenly the guns fell entirely silent, like dogs in the night, which, after keeping you awake for hours by their barking, suddenly decide to fall asleep instead. (17).

This description demonstrates the suddenness in which an air raid concludes and the havoc dissipates. As previously discussed, Nick and the other characters react to their dramatic situations in a similarly sudden sense: after moments of quick response, they return to the menial tasks of everyday life.

The third and final dramatic scene of the book involves Widmerpool and his meddling in military affairs. Throughout the book he has been attempting to have his chosen man appointed officer of the Recce Unit. He has also accused Diplock of embezzling money from the Division. These affairs reach a climax in the final pages of the book when Farebrother, Colonel Hogbourne-Johnson and the DAPM, Keef, visit Widmerpool's office. To Nick, "it [is] all at once clear as day that one of [Farebrother's] reasons for coming round to Div HA [is] to inform Widmerpool of this promotion to lieutenant-colonel" (198). Widmerpool counters by telling Farebrother that he will be going to the Cabinet Offices. At this point, Farebrother "brings out his trump card," and reveals that his choice, Ivo Deanery, has been appointed to the Recce Unit (202). Furthermore, he relays the message that "the MGA thinks [Widmerpool] is a bit too interested" in the Recce Unit affair and that "there's going to be a hell of a row" (203). Widmerpool, extremely defensive, "goes very red" and becomes "furious" (204).

While Widmerpool tries to recompose himself from this situation, Hogbourne-Johnson asks him to apologize for accusing Diplock of stealing money. Widmerpool ignores him, giving "the impression that his mind was on other things," such as his own fate in the army (211). The situation continues to escalate; Widmerpool may need to leave the army after his huge embarrassments. To his relief, however, Diplock deserts the army, proving him guilty and justifying Widmerpool's suspicions. The Widmerpool affair settles down as "there [is] nothing to be done" but "only wait and see how matters [shape]"(216). After the intensity and rapidity of these events, Nick goes back to F Mess for dinner (228).

The dramatic events of *The Soldier's Art* occur sporadically and with great intensity and thus resemble the air raids that punctuated life in England during World War II. Not necessarily frequent, these events at first shake up the people. Eventually, though, the raids become commonplace enough that people are able to quickly return to their regular lives. Nick notes, "It might be added that all sense of excitement was to evaporate from air-raids three or four years later" (17). In the course of this book, we see that this is truly that case. The final sentence of the book is: "That same week the plane was shot down in which Barnby was undertaking a reconnaissance flight with the aim of reporting on enemy camouflage" (228). The nonchalance with which Nick adds this onto his accounts in this book reveals that the dramatic events of his life during the war have become routine.

WRONG VOLUME: SILENCE AND NOISE REVERSED
DOUGLAS PRESLEY

War is loud. Bombs don't explode quietly and guns don't fire silently. Yet the most ominous sound in The *Soldier's Art* seems to be silence. The deafening noises of the war do not instill the damage that is expected of them; the situation always seems to turn out all right, despite the noise. When the volume turns soft or silent, however, the war seems to wreak its worst havoc. Silence – not noise – surrounds unhappiness and misfortune within the book.

When the *Luftwaffe* attacks, air raid sirens begin to blare. "The melancholy dirge of sirens, like ritual wailings at barbarous obsequies" (5) announces the arrival of the enemy planes, and once the attack has ceased, the "All Clear" sirens begin to sound. In addition to the sirens, the brens on the ground generate a "good deal of noise" (7). Nick describes the "noise of the cannonade" (11), as well as the "concentrated burst of ack-ack fire" (13) and the "clatter of the guns" (14) that cause Bithel so much difficulty in being heard. While the picture painted of these attacks is loud and grim, everyone seems to weather them, as there is no mention of death in the surrounding pages.

Nick also uses the cliché of "the rattle of musketry from distant hills" (15) to stir Bithel into further conversation about his boyhood aspirations. Once again, sound, while ominous and foreboding, turns out to be an ally, recalling for Bithel happy memories of reading childhood stories.

During the dinner with Moreland, Mrs. Maclintick, Stevens, and Priscilla, the characters cannot hear the air raid sirens announcing the blitz. When Priscilla thinks she hears the raid, she becomes "quite silent" (137). All the characters begin to listen but are unable to identify the noise of the sirens, and therefore simply ignore the warning. As it turns out, however, the raid they do not hear is the one that kills Chips. Later in the same dinner, Priscilla and Stevens begin to quarrel slightly when she claims to be sick. At first, Stevens tries to blame the headache on the restaurant being "noisy" (139). When things get really bad, however, it gets quiet. "There was silence for a moment. `I think I'll make for home,' [said Priscilla]" (140). She has only complained about a headache up till that moment, yet suddenly in the silence she decides to go home. Her decision is a fatal one, as she arrives at the house only to be killed in another raid.

Later in the book, silence is once again present in an unfortunate situation. When Keef reports to Colonel Hogbourne-Johnson that Diplock has deserted, the colonel can "find no words at first to register he fully comprehended what Keef had to report" (213). As Keef waits for a response, "the awfulness of the silence that follows" (213) wears on his nerves, until he breaks it to relieve the tension. Once again silence accompanies unfortunate situations, in this case even being directly described as "awful."

The noises of war, the booming guns and wailing sirens, accompany safety and security. When only silence or the normal hum of traffic is present, it is the lack of war noises that seems to bring misfortune. Powell has reversed the roles of sound and silence as we normally think of them; peace is not peaceful, and the real damage is done when all grows quiet.

©Douglas Presley, 2002

THE THEATRE OF WAR:
CIVILIAN AND MILITARY LIFE IN THE SOLDIER'S ART
PAUL MCCARTHY

The Soldier's Art begins with Nick purchasing his army greatcoat from a theatrical costume shop in London before going to join up with his regiment. As he's standing there, waiting to be served, he notices two dummies in a display case, one dressed in a "Harlequin's diagonally spangled tights; the other, scarlet full-dress uniform of some infantry regiment" (1). Nick at first describes these two as being polar opposites, symbols representing "Civil and Military ... Work and Play ... Detachment and Involvement ... Tragedy and Comedy ... War and Peace ... Life and Death...." The Harlequin is of the theatre, of leisure and happiness. He thrives in peacetime. The soldier is of the army, of violence and pain. He thrives in wartime. At first glance, these two images seem to live in completely different worlds, but, in reality, they do not. *The Soldier's Art* is full of instances where the military is connected to the theatre and to the civilian world, and the civilian world, in turn, is rife with violence and pain. As *The Soldier's Art* unfolds, and with it the events of World War II, these two worlds become more and more tangled together, until there is barely any difference.

After the costume shop scene, Nick shifts back to the present, when he is stationed at Divisional HQ, in the middle of a German air raid. The world "was dipped in a livid, unearthly refulgence, theatrical yet sinister" (12). By using the word "theatrical," Powell immediately links the war back to the theatre, to the civilian world, suggesting that the two might not be as far apart as Nick first imagined. And, then, as the raid is going on, Nick decides to take a walk with Bithel and discuss a bounced check Bithel had written, while bombs are dropping on the HQ. Nothing about that scene is particularly military in nature. Actually, the conversation would have made more sense set in a London office or on the way to a business meeting, not on a field of war. And, later on, Widmerpool says with respect to Stringham, "We are none of us called upon to do more than fulfill the duties of our respective ranks and appointments, vegetables or no vegetables." Both of these instances make the military seem much less serious and dangerous: after all, if people have enough time to talk about finances on a battlefield, or to gripe about dealing with vegetables, then they are probably not in eminent danger.

As a matter of fact, the only time we see Nick's regiment acting like a military force is during their "schemes," or war games, where the two sides are denoted as "Blue Force" and "Red Force" (33). But this "battle" seems to be play-acting as much as anything else. No one dies; there are no tactical gains or losses in the grand scheme of things, just practice. And so, even the most dangerous, important parts of Nick's time at Div HQ are little more than an overly complicated theatrical performance.

There are also a couple of explicit references to theatre during Nick's time at the Divisional HQ. Chapter 2 opens with a theatre metaphor, comparing the division to an acting troupe in the process of rehearsing for a play, or, in this case, the war (88). Also, Sergeant Ablett, one of the soldiers in the Mobile Laundry Unit, is a former vaudeville comedian, famous for his "trouserless tap-dance"(224). His presence adds to the idea of theatre combining with the military.

These moments of relative peace and comedy in the military are put into stark contrast with the bleak and dangerous world that civilian London has now become. Most of the old nightclubs that Nick once frequented are closed, and those that are still open are much more subdued in nature. Chips Lovell says that the Café Madrid will be "a very sober affair compared with the old days" (115). Moreland and Audrey have to cope with the hassles of ration cards and blackouts, and, of course, the ever-present danger of air raids. This last danger is made especially apparent with the deaths of Chips and Priscilla Lovell during a pair of air raids. And it is that night, the night that the Café Madrid is destroyed, that we get the first real hero of *The Soldier's Art*.

Max Pilgrim, an actor, a singer, helps drags seven people out of the Madrid's wreckage (156). That is far and away the bravest thing anyone does in the entire book, and not a military hero or a soldier, but a civilian actor does it. Based on the events of that night, the tragedy of the Lovells and the heroism of Max Pilgrim, along with the rather mundane happenings at Div HQ, it seems civilian life has become more harrowing than military life, and the two worlds, the civilian and the military, aren't as separate as Nick originally thought, when he looked at those two dummies.

Immediately following that first visual in the costume shop, the clerk comes out of the storeroom with Nick's greatcoat. He then mistakes Nick for an actor in a play called *The War*. Then Nick starts thinking about how accurate a metaphor the theatre really is for a war. By the time he turns to leave, he has completely changed his opinion. "On second thought, the headless figures were perhaps not antithetical at all" (4). That moment sets up a basis for all that follows it: the relationship between the theatre and the war, the civilian world and the military one, and how, over the course of World War II, they became so mixed that they might as well be one and the same.

CHILDE STRINGHAM TO THE DARK TOWER CAME:
FORESHADOWING STRINGHAM'S DEATH
MICHAEL DONELAN

> I shut my eyes and turn'd them on my heart.
> As a man calls for wine before he fights,
> I ask'd one draught of earlier, happier sights
> Ere fitly I could hope to play my part.
> Think first, fight afterwards – the soldier's art:
> One taste of the old time sets all to rights.
> $\qquad$ - Robert Browning

A Soldier's Art brings us back in touch with one of our good friends, Charles Stringham. Nick is very surprised to find Stringham serving him potatoes one night in F Mess and is happy – though uncomfortable – to have reconnected with him. Shortly after their first encounter we see that Stringham has become a wholly different individual, one that does not want to remember days past. During Nick's last conversation with him, on page 221, he reads a single stanza from Robert Browning's *Childe Roland to the Dark Tower Came*, reprinted above. Stringham declares that the poem "has about twenty different meanings" (221). One of them is that this stanza foreshadows the death that awaits him as soon as he and the Mobile Laundry Unit are shipped off to the East.

In the first couplet, we see Stringham struggle to redefine himself in his sobriety and his new role in the army. Browning's stanza begins, "I shut my eyes and turned them on my heart. / As a man calls for wine before he fights." He is attempting to shift through his tumultuous life to find meaning, and what he has found is the ritualism and structure of the army to give himself purpose. Stringham is reflecting as if these are his last moments of introspection before he heads into battle knowing he is going to die. The reference to wine alludes to Stringham's fight with alcoholism before joining the army.

The alcoholism is again referred to in the third line of the stanza, "I asked one draught of earlier, happier sights," reminding the reader of times that Stringham was dependent upon drink. Now that he has regained his sobriety, he realizes, "even I myself grasped I'd become the most desperate of bores by being permanently sober" (80). The "one draught" refers to the drinks that he would consume at earlier parties, which were happier sights for everyone, Stringham enjoying his drunken stupor and all those he entertained reaping the hilarious benefits of his intoxication.

In the forth line of the stanza we move away from events past and towards current ones. Stringham reads, "Ere fitly I could hope to play my part" (221). When the war came along, "I began to develop all sorts of martial ambitions ... The long and the short of it was, I entered the army" (80). War being brought upon England leads him to sign up for the army so that he can play his part, or at least feel as though he is doing so. Early in this encounter, Nick asks Stringham if he and Widmerpool can "find something better" for him. At this suggestion he is almost offended. Nick responds awkwardly, "I don't know. I thought there might be something" (76). His voice full of rueful irony, Stringham says he has the talent to do well as a waiter. "It's just a question of developing latent ability. I never dreamed I possessed such potentialities. It's been marvelous to release them" (77). This is Stringham's idea of playing his part in the war. At first he has no desire to relinquish his duties as F Mess waiter. Later, when it comes time for the Mobile Laundry Unit to be shipped to the Far East, Nick asks if he will go through with this relocation. Stringham answers, "Not a doubt" (220); and the move ultimately leads to his death.

This book's title is taken from the stanza's fifth line, "Think first, fight afterwards - the soldier's art." This is why Stringham joined the army in the first place, taken by the glorified ideal of fighting and dying for his country. "Fell in action. I'm always struck by that phrase" (78), he says when talking about Robert Tolland dying in battle. It gives him meaning. He has already done his thinking in life, and now he can finally do his fighting to die in the army.

The last line in the stanza "One taste of the old time sets all to rights" is the defining piece that leads one to conclude this poem foreshadows Stringham's now imminent death. Old memories are revisited one last time during Nick and Stringham's last meeting. The two have caught up with one another, bringing closure to their relationship, tying the strings and things between them are reconciled. It is finally time for Stringham to fulfill his destiny as indicated in the poem and die valiantly for his country in the name of the soldier's art.

©Michael Donelan, 2008

CHAPTER 9:
THE MILITARY PHILOSOPHERS

The Military Philosophers marked the beginning of our third term of *Dance*, and thus we picked up some new travelers. It was perhaps an easier place to begin than *Casanova's Chinese Restaurant* was for the second term newcomers. The war ends – a more familiar setting for most of the students than the Depression music scene. Here they found topics to get their teeth into: the Katyn massacre, which sparked two papers; the deaths of Nick's two oldest friends, Stringham and Templer; and the dreadful Pamela Flitton. Five of the students wrote about her, and all of them were transfixed by her meanness. "Black Widow," Becca Zinsmeister called her, and everyone else agreed.

After the personal pressure Nick Jenkins has been experiencing under Widmerpool, his transfer to Finn's section and his association with the agreeable David Pennistone comes as a relief. We find more humor here than in the last book: Blackhead the apparatchik, Mrs. Erdleigh the seer, Szymanski the scoundrel, and Pamela the Scourge of God. Even the last scene is a joke, as – the great war at an end – Nick and Archie Gilbert, that former "'spare man' *par excellence*," pick out their demob outfits, taking everything. "Except the underclothes."

One student, as I mentioned in the Introduction, compiled an extraordinarily useful glossary of the military acronyms that run (like cockroaches, I think) through the war trilogy. I have often thanked Will Story *in absentia* for having undertaken this task, especially when I taught the books the second time through. It was a vast and collaborative undertaking; Will used the Anthony Powell Society's list-serve to help resolve impasses. I remember his having a difficult time with ATS, the letters that describe driver Pamela Flitton. "Army Transport Service" seemed so logical to all of us – but it was wrong. "Auxiliary Territorial Service" was the answer: "Auxiliary" because it was female, and "Territorial" because it was a domestic service rather than foreign (as Widmerpool's "Territorials," which we in the USA would call National Guard). Will worked well past the deadline on this project, refining it after it had been put on the web. He and I – and everyone else that uses this resource – are grateful to all those who contributed their knowledge to this project.

The Military Philosophers begins in 1942. Jenkins is working with Pennistone under Finn as liaison with the Poles. At a meeting to discuss the release of thousands of Polish officers from Russia, he runs into Widmerpool, Farebrother, and Templer. Through work he later has dealings with Blackhead, a bureaucrat of the highest degree. Pamela Flitton, Stringham's niece and an Auxiliary Territorial driver, takes Jenkins to various meetings around London. From her we learn of Stringham's death as a POW in Singapore.

Norah Tolland brings Pamela to Ted Jeavons's party. At work, Jenkins meets Kucherman, a Belgian attaché, and learns that Szymanski – a mythologically difficult Polish officer – has escaped from detention barracks. With Isobel, he attends *The Bartered Bride*, where Pamela turns up. Widmerpool, also present, asks about her. Others speak of her notoriety concerning numerous sexual conquests. Widmerpool becomes a full colonel.

Jenkins meets Pamela and Odo Stevens at an air raid shelter. Mrs. Erdleigh turns up and is eager to read Pamela's palm, predicting marriage to "a man a little older." When Stevens tries to stop Pamela from going outside during the raid, she slaps him. Mrs. Erdleigh reports the death of Dr. Trelawney.

Finn and Jenkins conduct the various military attaches to France for a tour. When Maj. Prasad says he requires a bathroom "for religious reasons," Jenkins must request that Gen. Asbjørnsen yield his room. Jenkins runs into his former Welsh unit, commanded now by Kedward, who remembers him with difficulty. The Field-Marshal gives the attaches an audience, and lectures the Belgians about their Resistance fighters, who are causing the Allies difficulty. Jenkins has a drink with Bob Duport, and learns that Templer has been killed.

As the War winds down in the Pacific theater, Jenkins's fellow officers begin to return to civilian life. He reads of the engagement between Pamela Flitton and Widmerpool and later attends a party at Prasad's Embassy with Isobel, where he meets

Widmerpool and Pamela, Sunny Farebrother and his new wife "Tuffy" Weedon (widow of General Conyers), and Matilda Wilson with her husband Sir Magnus Donners. Pamela and Widmerpool argue whether Widmerpool was responsible for Templer's death. At the St. Paul's celebration of the end of the war, Nick allows Colonel Flores to take his seat and meets Jean Templer, now Sra. Flores, again for the first time in several years. The book ends with an unexpected meeting with Archie Gilbert, the cosmopolitan partygoer from *A Buyer's Market*.

CHARACTER LIST

The major characters in this volume, arranged by chapter:

Chapter 1

Lt. Col. (Lysander) Finn – head of military liaison at the War Office
Maj. David Penniston – colleague of Jenkins in military liaison
Blackhead – obstructionist civil servant
Lt. Col. Widmerpool – heads a committee in Cabinet Office
Lt. Col. Sunny Farebrother – involved in military espionage
Peter Templer - old friend of Jenkins, working in MEW
Pamela Flitton - AT driver, niece of Charles Stringham
Prince Theodoric - Baltic prince

Chapter 2

Ted Jeavons – ARP warden, widower
Norah Tolland – Jenkins's sister-in-law
Major Kucherman – Belgian military attaché
Isobel - Jenkins's wife

Chapter 3

Maj. Odo Stevens - "secret show" officer, acquaintance of Jenkins
Mrs. Myra Erdleigh - fortune-teller, friend of Jenkins's late uncle

Chapter 4

Major Prasad – Indian military attaché
Gen. Asbjørnsen – Scandinavian military attaché
Various other attachés
The Field-Marshal – Bernard Montgomery (historical figure)
Capt. Idwal Kedward – CO of Jenkins's former Welch company

Capt. Bob Duport –former brother-in-law of Peter Templer

Chapter 5

Geraldine "Tuffy" Weedon Farebrother - Sunny's new wife, MI5
Col. Flores - South American military attaché
Jean Templer Duport Flores - Jenkins's old heart-throb

* * *

Haiku

Nick did not expect
That on that day he would see
Señora Flores.
        - Madeleine Fawcett

High up in the eves
Bureaucrat extraordinaire
Blackhead waits for prey.
        - Doug Presley

A polite request;
Please amplify, notes on soap:
Blackhead is not pleased.
        - Luke Spears

LEARNING THE ABC OF MILITARY AFFAIRS
WILL STORY

This glossary of all the military abbreviations in the war trilogy of *Dance* is set up in alphabetical order. The abbreviations, each with definition, are given, followed by the first book and page number that it appears. The book abbreviations are *VB* (*The Valley of Bones*), *SA* (*The Soldier's Art*), and *MP* (*The Military Philosophers*).

A

ACI: Army Council Instruction, *SA* 60
ADC: Aide-de-Camp, *VB* 93
A & Q: Adjutant & Quartermaster, *SA* 22
ARP: Air Raid Precautions, *MP* 75
AT: Auxiliary Territorial, *MP* 33
ATS: Auxiliary Territorial Service, *MP* 34

B

Battalion HQ: Battalion Head Quarters, *VB* 80

C

CB: Confined to barracks, *VB* 62
CBE: Commander of the Order of the British Empire, *MP* 228
CD: Corps Diplomat, *MP* 232
C of E: Church of England, *VB* 20
CIGS: Chief of Imperial General Staff, *SA* 80
CO: Commanding Officer, *VB* 15
CRA: Commander, Royal Artillery, *SA* 28
CRASC: Commanding Royal Army Service Corps, *SA* 62
CQMS: Company Quartermaster Sergeant, *VB* 176
CSM: Company Sergeant-Major, *VB* 6

D

DAAG: Deputy Assistant Adjutant General, *VB* 222
DADMS: Deputy Assistant Director Medical Services, *SA* 65
DAPM: Deputy Assistant Provost Marshal, *SA* 54
DCO: Divisional Catering Officer, *SA* 64
Div HQ: Divisional Headquarters, *VB* 194
DR: Dispatch Rider, *SA* 55
DSC: Distinguished Service Cross, *VB* 162
DSD: Director of Staff Duties, *MP* 195
DSO: Distinguished Service Order, *SA* 196

E

ENSA: Entertainment's National Service Association, *SA* 116

F

FSO: Field Security Officer, *SA* 59

G

GHQ: General Headquarters, *MP* 46
GOC: General Officer Commanding, *MP* 17

I

ITC: Infantry training Centre, *VB* 169

L

LAD: Light Aid Detachment, *SA* 57
L of C Captain: Lines of Communication Captain, *MP* 172

M

MA: Military Attaché, *MP* 86
MBE: Member of the Order of the British Empire, *MP* 239
MC: Military Cross, *VB* 50

MEW: Ministry of Economic Warfare, *MP* 15
MI5: Military Intelligence 5 (secret service), *MP* 73
MGA: Major-General in charge of Administration, *SA* 199
MM: Military Medal, *SA* 60
MO: Medical Officer, *VB* 82
MP: Military Police, *VB* 112
MS Officer: Military Secretariat Officer, *MP* 240
MT: Motor Transport, *VB* 10

N

NCO: Non-commissioned Officer, *VB* 18

O

OBE: Officer of the Order of the British Empire, *SA* 196
OC: Officer in Charge, *SA* 217
OCTU: Officer Cadet Training Unit, *SA* 44

P

PM: Prime Minister, *MP* 20
PLUTO: Pipe Line Under the Ocean, *MP* 155
POW: Prisoner of War, *MP* 204
PT: Physical Training *VB* 71

Q

QM: Quartermaster *VB* 10
Q (Ops.): Quartermaster Operations, *MP* 30

R

RAF: Royal Air Force, *VB* 19
RAOC: Royal Army Ordnance Corps, *VB* 157
RASC: Royal Army Service Corps, *SA* 62
RC: Roman Catholic, *VB* 20
RAMC: Royal Army Medical Corps, *MP* 103

RMC: Royal Military College, *MP* 55
RTO: Railway Transport Officer, *VB* 142
RV: Rendezvous, *VB* 77

S

SOPT: Staff Officer, Physical Training, *SA* 69

T

TA Reservist-Territorial Army Reservist: *VB* 35

V

VC-Victoria Cross: *VB* 14
VD-Venereal Disease: *SA* 66

W

WOASAWL-While-On-Active-Service-Absent-Without-Leave: *SA* 149
W/T: Wireless Telephone, *SA*, 42

Thanks to the following for their contributions:
Julian Allason, Nick Birns, John Gilks, Dr. Keith C. Marshall, Nick Nash, Philip Stokes, and (as will be apparent below) Michael Skaife d'Ingerthorpe.

Letter from Michael Skaife d'Ingerthorpe

I was impressed by Will Story's ABC in *The Military Philosophers* section and especially by his getting CBE right, viz. Commander of the Order of the British Empire; this sort of thing is often got wrong in this country (England). However, I was then disappointed that he made the usual sort of mistake regarding the equivalent OBE and MBE. Just in case anyone's interested, it goes like this (from lowest to highest rank):

MBE – Member of the Order of the British Empire
OBE – Officer of the Order of the British Empire
CBE – Commander of the Order of the British Empire
KBE or DBE – Knight Commander or Dame Commander of the Order of the British Empire
GBE – Knight Grand Cross or Dame Grand Cross of the Order of the British Empire

There are similar (though not identical) gradations for other orders.

(I can take some comfort in presuming to correct you on this sort of thing, from the fact that AP was evidently also liable to be annoyed by mistakes of this sort!)

With best wishes and in admiration of what I've seen of the site and certainly of the enterprise as a whole,

Michael Skaife d'Ingerthorpe

(Note: Michael's corrections to Will's "Learning the ABC of Military Affairs" have been added to his text. Will, the rest of the class, and I are all grateful for Michael's expertise.)

Above and Below Ground:
Nick's Place in the Army
John Bukawyn

In the corporate world of America, Britain, and elsewhere, the general consensus seems to be the higher up you sit, the more illustrious your job. During World War II, however, the order is completely reversed. Due to the constant blitzes and arrivals of V1s, and V2s, living or working towards the top of a building meant greater risk of being blown up. In *The Military Philosophers*, this is the case. By placing important and secret work below ground and less meaningful tidbits near the top, the British army took measures to protect itself from serious blows. In this hierarchy, Nick Jenkins seems to be right in the middle: above some, but also below many.

As Nick climbs the stairs to the higher levels, on which live "the Civil branches and their subsidiaries, Finance, Internal Administration, Passive Air Defence, all diminishing in official prestige as the altitude steepened," (38) he prepares himself for Blackhead. Blackhead, one of the most infamous characters in *The Military Philosophers*, deals with simple issues yet is a huge nuisance to get through. Nick brings to his attention the matter of "restrictions on straw for hospital palliasses" (38) in Scotland. This issue may be irrelevant to the war being fought on continental Europe, but for Blackhead it requires much thought. In fact it is by no means the only unimportant material that he deals with. Whether it is the Belgian Women's Corps looking for a bicycle or the Norwegian military attaché seeking office furniture, requisitions must go through Blackhead's office (42). Placed in "a rookery of lesser activities" (38) near the attic of Nick's building, Blackhead's work is relatively insignificant, far from any truly important business.

On the opposite side of the spectrum, in the basement, imperative, high security matters are discussed. Nick replaces

Pennistone, his senior officer, to sit in on a meeting to discuss the release of Polish officers from Russia. On his way there he describes his surroundings, saying that a marine, "showed [him] into a room in the bowels of earth ... a brightly lit dungeon" (11-12). Sunny Farebrother makes similar comments: "Can't tell whether it's three o'clock in the morning, or three o'clock in the afternoon. No disturbance from time" (14). Nick and Farebrother are so far beneath ground that neither sun nor bomb penetrates into the basement, making it a timeless and safe place to conduct serious and important business. Once Widmerpool enters the room, the men begin to discuss the matters at hand. Once the issue of the Poles has concluded, some men, including Nick, are required to leave with Widmerpool's snide comments: "I have some highly secretive matters to deal with on the next agenda. I can't begin on them with people like you hanging about the room" (16). Here Widmerpool illustrates the importance of the topics discussed in the basements of buildings.

With a second floor office, Nick is physically located between the two opposing extremes, halfway between Blackhead's perch and Widmerpool's dungeon. Working with the Poles and later the Belgians, Nick's own agenda simply seems more important than Blackhead's soap issues, but also less important than Widmerpool's sensitive affairs. By discussing the matter of straw with Blackhead and also conversing about the Poles with Widmerpool, Nick shows that he is the middleman, moving between the little people up high and the giants below.

THE KATYN MASSACRE
NICOLE LEE

In *The Military Philosophers*, Jenkins hears an announcement on the German radio, "stating that a place called Katyn, near the Russian town of Smolensk, an accumulation of communal graves has been found by advancing German troops" (102). Thousands of corpses in Polish uniforms were placed on top of each other with their hands tied together and a bullet through the backs of their heads. "The source of this information was naturally suspect, but, if in any degree to be believed, offered one solution to the mysterious disappearance of the untraced ten or fifteen thousand Polish officers, made prisoners of war by the Soviet army in 1939" (103). This description in *A Dance to the Music of Time* very accurately reflects the Katyn massacre that occurred in World War II.

In September 1939, Germany invaded Poland. The Soviets soon after came to occupy eastern Poland and interned thousands of Poles. After the German invasion of the Soviet Union in 1941, the Polish government agreed to cooperate with Soviets against Germany. The Polish general who was forming the new army asked to have the Polish prisoners under his command, but was told that (in December 1941) most had already escaped to Manchuria and had disappeared. In December 1943, the Germans discovered the mass graves of these servicemen in the Katyn forest in western Russia.

The disappearance of these men remained a mystery until many years after the actual massacre. In the spring of 1940, over 4,000 prisoners of war were taken out to the forest to be killed in small groups. They were taken in greatcoats with their hands tied behind their back, placed face down upon the fresh corpses of their fellow servicemen and shot through the back of the head. Those who resisted had self-strangulation knots tied from their hands to necks. Those who screamed had sawdust forced down their throats. Their mass graves of these men who were only thought to be missing were found in April 1943 by the Nazi government. The Germans said they found a ditch 28 meters long and 16 meters wide at the Hill of Goats, with all of the bodies dressed in full military uniform piled in layers of twelve. The soil had preserved their bodies and their documentation.

The initial response of the Russians to the Germans' claim was that the Germans committed this act themselves. The Allies were fighting the Nazis, and Russia was an ally, so the German version was not accepted by any of the Allied governments. Any information made public during this time came from Joseph Goebbels, the German propaganda minister, and was treated as suspect by the Allies. In January 1943, the Russians had defeated the Germans at Stalingrad so any criticism about them was not readily accepted. A relation between the Germans and the massacre became popular by all those fighting the Nazis. In the Cold War era, the Russian version was finally brought into question and found to be false.

Besides the 4,000 men killed in this forest, the Katyn massacre also refers to the 10,000 others murdered at the same time. These included 4000 at the Starobielsk Camp and 6000 at the Ostashkow camp. It was noted that as men left the Starobielsk camp, each daily group had been selected from many different prison blocks and never included groups of friends. One report states that while the Germans were later being driven back from the Kharkov area, Russian shells were bursting north of the town. One barrage of shells "caused corpses to fly in the air, as if from some burial ground." There was no further investigation of this sentence, until of course years later when the mass graves were found. The victims of this horrible massacre were Polish officers and cadets that held professions such as doctors, lawyers, teachers and clergymen. They were considered the "best and the brightest" of Polish society.

In *A Dance to the Music of Time*, Jenkins' own personal view of the Katyn massacre can be inferred from the reactions of the characters in this novel. Since Powell himself worked with the Poles, it would only make sense that he was upset by the massacre. In his memoirs, he says, "at this period it was thought by the London Poles that the missing officers had been exiled to distant camps within the Arctic Circle. Their atrocious massacre by the Russians at Katyn was to emerge only later" (Powell 144). In *The Military Philosophers*, on the day this news was released, Nick was going to see Finn about some matter and found him to be "in one of his unapproachable moods" because the "Russo-Polish situation had thoroughly upset him" (103). The reaction of Finn seems most similarly to parallel that of Jenkins'.

Not all the characters, however, are sympathetic to the Poles and angry with the Russians. Widmerpool says, "Just because these deaths are very upsetting to the Poles themselves ... it's no reason to undermine the fabric of our alliances against the Axis" (106). He then finishes off the conversation by mentioning that it is not worth while to pay attention to "the interests of a few thousand Polish exiles, who, however worthy their cause, cannot properly handle their diplomatic relations" (107). Although this reaction is directly opposite what one may expect from Powell, he has somewhat prepared us for this reaction. Particularly in this book and throughout the last few, Widmerpool has set off on a power trip and continuously becomes a generally disliked character. An online critical essay by Christopher Caldwell summarizes this by saying, "it is characteristic of Widmerpool's can-do attitude that he hates the Poles for raising a fuss about the Katyn Forest massacre." Overall, Powell accurately portrays the gruesome details of Katyn massacre and expresses his own feelings through his characters.

Sources:

1. Caldwell, Christopher. "Anthony Powell's Century; Britain's novelist of manners turns 100." 2005. http://www.encyclopedia.com/doc/1G1-143832513.html 12 Apr 2008

2. Coatney, Louis Robert. *The Katyn Massacre: An Assessment of its Significance as a Public and Historical Issue in the United*

States and Great Britain, 1940-1993: A Thesis Presented to the Department of History, Western Illinois University. December 1993.
3. *The Journal of Historical Review*. Vol. 1, no. 1. 31-42 http://www.vho.org/GB/Journals/JHR/1/1/FitzGibbon31-42.html 11 Apr 2008
4. "Katyn Massacre." *Britannica Concise Encyclopedia*. 2007. http://www.encyclopedia.com/doc/1B1-368977.html 11 Apr 2008
5. Powell, Anthony. *Faces in My Time*. New York. 1980.
6. Trueman, Chris. "The Katyn Wood Massacre." *History Learning Site*. 2000-2008. http://www.historylearningsite.co.uk/katyn_wood_massacre.html 12 Apr 2008

PAMELA FLITTON: THE BLACK WIDOW
BECCA ZINSMEISTER

The soon-to-be infamous Pamela Flitton makes her debut in *The Military Philosophers*, paving her way with trampled hearts and bruised egos. A woman always in control, she takes great pleasure in making those graced by her presence uncomfortable. In the first description of Pamela, we learn of her beauty, but Nick later states that there is something "unnatural" about her (60). This statement gains more credibility as our knowledge of Pamela's character grows.

Through first-hand observation beginning with Pamela chauffeuring Nick about the city, we discover her unpleasant disposition. During their drive her reluctance to converse and her disregard for acceptable social niceties creates unnecessary tension between them. This attitude is later carried over to the party at Ted Jeavons's residence. Here we first witness her in a social setting, where she proceeds to ignore her date – Nick's sister-in-law Norah Tolland – and sit in the corner, rebuffing all attempts at conversation. Her actions show a complete disregard for the people around her and the lack of concern she has for their feelings. When leaving the party, Pamela asks Nick about the Syzmanski affair, which is her only attempt at being social the entire night. In fact, here she seems almost pleasant, even laughing jovially at Nick's words. Yet, obviously her goal is to gain information about a subject she is interested in, not to be sociable (82).

As the book unfolds, our impressions of Pamela's character continue to worsen as her cruel nature reveals itself during her exchange with Odo Stevens and Nick. Throughout the conversation she strives to put down Stevens as many times as possible saying, "You have the weakest head out of any man I have ever met" (125) or "You're pathetic as a lover" (135). She purposely makes disparaging remarks in front of other people, because she wants to embarrass Stevens. Due to the frequency of these comments, her behavior takes a more sadistic tone. She even resorts to violence, striking Stevens across the face, when he dares to question her actions.

Odo Stevens, like many others, boasts a place on Pamela's list of conquests. We learn through word of mouth that Pamela is to blame for Peter Templer's recent bout with depression, forcing him to prove his youth and vigor, disastrously resulting in his death. Clearly Pamela Flitton enjoys preying on the insecurities of others. In his prime Templer had success in his love life, being the first of his friends to lose his virginity. However, then he suffers through two failed marriages, most likely inspiring some self-doubt. Enter Pamela, who after some sort of relationship with Templer casts him off in search of more tender meat.

The engagement between Widmerpool and Pamela shocks Nick and many others because of their seemingly odd pairing. Yet, Widmerpool is Pamela's ultimate challenge. Here is a man hungry for power, who enjoys showing off his successes to his colleagues. Pamela makes it her business to take the men she is involved with and destroy them from the inside out. It seems that Widmerpool has further to fall than her previous conquests. Unlike Templer, however, Widmerpool is resilient, quickly rising to the top and easily moving around obstacles. He has successfully moved past his embarrassing previous engagement to Mildred Haycock and it will be much more difficult for Pamela to truly harm him.

At the National Day party we see first-hand the dynamics of Widmerpool and Pamela's relationship. She arrives late, dressed, according to Nick, "in the most filthy garments she possessed," displaying indifference toward her environment (209). In addition, she refuses to allow Widmerpool to introduce her to high-ranking officials, denying him the chance to show off his status. She even demands that he skip dinner with the minister. Unlike Stevens, he refuses to give in to her demands and despite a heated argument sticks to his plans. This decision may have led to her deliberately trying to humiliate him by calling him a "murderer," and then by refusing to drop the subject of Templer's death, knowing full well that someone could overhear her remarks (213).

Given the dispositions of both Widmerpool and Pamela, their marriage cannot possibly be a happy or a long one. Both bolster their egos by putting down those around them and then climbing above them. Ultimately, Pamela will probably either grow tired of Widmerpool or finally succeed in ruining him.

©Rebecca Zinsmeister, 2008

CHAPTER 10:
BOOKS DO FURNISH A ROOM

At last, after examining the arts of music, of painting, and of theater in 20th-century Britain, *Dance* arrives at literature. Nick explicitly tells us about the task of writing books, as he settles down to work on *Hellebore and Borage*, his biography of Robert Burton. Quiggin and Craggs publish books, as well as the "little" magazine *Fission*. And X. Trapnel – explicitly modeled on Julian Maclaren-Ross – lives out the existence of a starving Bohemian writer, his never-to-be published magnum opus, *Profiles in String*, destroyed by the Fury-like Pamela Widmerpool, no Kindly One Pam. Everyone is writing. Sillery is preparing to release his diaries. Even Odo Stevens publishes *Sad Majors* – and to a warm critical reception.

The students enjoyed *Books Do Furnish a Room*, found much of it amusing, although they were aware of its somber elements as well. Nick Anschuetz wrote a sensitive response to its opening, where Nick Jenkins deals with a bout of post-war depression. Will Story took a look at the humor of Erridge's funeral. And Alex Svec, inspired by my having read aloud Maclaren-Ross's "So Long, My Buddy" – itself a parody of Raymond Chandler – produced a brilliant monologue of the private detective Widmerpool hired to track down Pamela and Trapnel.

One other stand-out piece of work: Cassidy Carpenter, who earlier deduced that Nick and Powell share the same birthday (*A Buyer's Market*) looked closely at Jean Templer Duport Flores's Dior wardrobe, and deduced that the action must happen a year later than everyone (including Hillary Spurling and Powell himself) had realized/remembered

Synopsis

Books Do Furnish a Room begins at the "University" (Oxford) in 1945. After the War, Jenkins begins researching a book on Robert Burton and *The Anatomy of Melancholy*. He meets with Short and his old don Sillery, whose attractive secretary, Ada Leintwardine, is preparing the latter's journals for publication. He learns that Erridge has died, and he must return home for the funeral. On the train to London he runs into "Books" Bagshaw, who informs him about the magazine *Fission* and its publishers, Quiggin and Craggs.

The whole Tolland family including the Jenkinses attend Erridge's funeral. As the service is beginning, Widmerpool, Gypsy Jones Craggs, Craggs, Quiggin, Uncle Alfred Tolland, and Pamela enter. Pamela feels sick and, as she leaves, disrupts the service. Afterwards, at Erridge's living quarters at Thrubworth, the family and visitors discuss Erridge's affairs. Just before she leaves the house, Pamela vomits into a large oriental vase. Dicky Umfraville hints that he may be Pamela's father.

Jenkins goes to a party at the Flores's, where he realizes Jean is now rich. Rosie Manasch reveals that she has been funding *Fission*. Widmerpool arrives and hears Jenkins's plans to meet X. Trapnel. The next week they do so, with Bagshaw, and discuss many literary ideas. Jenkins runs into Moreland. At a *Fission* party, Odo Stevens sees Pamela, who looks right through him. Trapnel meets the Widmerpools. He seems disinterested in Pamela, but manages to borrow a pound from her husband.

At a pub Trapnel confesses to Jenkins his love for Pamela. Jenkins has dinner with Roddy Cutts; they meet Widmerpool and accompany him to his flat, where Short, who lives downstairs, tells them Pamela has left, perhaps with Trapnel. Trapnel, living with Pamela, writes a parody of Widmerpool for *Fission*. Later, while Nick is visiting Trapnel and Pamela at their squalid flat, Widmerpool appears and confronts them.

Jenkins returns to "School" (Eton) to make arrangements for his son to attend school there. Then, a flashback describes the collapse of *Fission* and the falling out between Pamela and Trapnel. As Bagshaw and Jenkins console Trapnel and take him home from a pub, they find the manuscript of his new novel *Profiles in String* (flung by Pamela) in the canal. Crushed, Trapnel hurls his walking stick into the water. Back at School, Jenkins meets Le Bas, who does not remember him, and then Widmerpool, who is vacationing with Pamela (who has returned to him). The book ends with a description of newly published books, which includes one of Jenkins's.

CHARACTER LIST

The major characters in this volume, arranged by chapter:

Chapter 1

Sillery – an elderly don
Leonard Short – a university contemporary of Jenkins
Ada Leintwardine – Sillery's secretary
"Books (Do Furnish a Room)" Bagshaw – proposed editor for *Fission*

Chapter 2

Hugo, Frederica, Norah, Blanche, Isobel – members of Tolland family
Alfred Tolland - uncle of Tollands
Kenneth Widmerpool - now a Member of Parliament
Pamela Flitton Widmerpool – his dangerous and awful wife
Gypsy Jones Craggs – one-time lover of Widmerpool, communist
Howard Craggs – publisher, married to Gypsy
Quiggin – old acquaintance of Jenkins, now publishing *Fission*
Mona – Peter Templer's ex-wife
Dickie Umfraville – Frederica Tolland's husband
Roddy Cutts – Susan Tolland's once-wandering husband

Chapter 3

X. Trapnel (Francis Xavier) – a well-regarded, perennially poor writer
Rosie Manasch – a friend from Jenkins's dancing days
Odo Stevens - acquaintance of Jenkins from the war
Col. Flores - South American military/governmental figure
Jean Templer Duport Flores - his wife, Jenkins's old heart-throb

Chapter 4

Evadne Clapham – a writer

Chapter 5

Le Bas – Jenkins's old housemaster when he attended "School"

Nick's Anatomy of Melancholy
Nicholas Anschuetz

The beginning of Anthony Powell's *Books Do Furnish a Room* marks the first time in three books in which we see Nick out of wartime. Hitler has been defeated and Japan obliterated. However, a time of rejoicing for England is a time of depression for Nick. His melancholy is apparent from the first sentence: "Reverting to the university at forty, one immediately recaptured all the crushing melancholy of the undergraduate condition" (1). As Nick writes his biography of Robert Burton, his depression at the beginning of the novel can be attributed to the combined effect of his irresolution, his presence at Oxford, and his loss during wartime.

According to Nick, "War left, on the one hand, a passionate desire to tackle a lot of work: on the other, never to do any work again... Irresolution appealed to [Robert Burton] as one of the myriad forms of Melancholy" (2). After the war, Nick had nothing to do. His military job abruptly ended and he was forced to adjust to civilian life after six years as a soldier. Even for a non-combatant soldier, it is a difficult transition. "Only a week before, the peak of a French general's khaki képi ... had by conditioned reflex jerked my right hand from its overcoat pocket in preparation for a no longer consonant salute" (1). We can see how it could be especially hard for Nick to revert to his old lifestyle because he did not really have a specific job to which he could return. After six years of uninterrupted work, it is easy to understand why he would want either to do nothing at all, or to work only at what he loves to do. Nick obviously wants to get back into writing, but writing is the sort of job that is easy to neglect if one procrastinates. His irresolution to work or not is part of the cause of his depression at the beginning of *Books Do Furnish a Room.*

At the beginning of the novel, we learn that Nick is revisiting University to do research for his biography of Robert Burton, and his presence there is another major cause for his depression. Powell promotes the image of Nick almost suffocating in the scholarly air, and Nick reminds himself what it was like to be an undergraduate student, not having any fun. "As the train drew up at the platform, before the local climate had time to impair health, academic contacts disturb the spirit, a more imminent gloom was re-established, its sinewy grip in a flash making one young again. Depressive symptoms, menacing in all haunts of youth, were in any case easily aroused at this period" (1). As students, we are familiar with the academic pressure about which Nick is talking.

Nick's depression can lastly be attributed to the loss of his friends during World War II. Although Nick says, "The odd thing was how distant the recent past had also become," he still acknowledges that "shades from those days still walked abroad" (1). During the war, he lost his uncle, his two oldest friends, his sister-in-law, his brother-in-law, and many, many more. The three World War II novels are the darkest of any of the books in the *A Dance to the Music of Time* series so far, and Nick, with nothing else to occupy his mind, is feeling this sorrow now. With the loss of so many people who were so close to him, the only people left are people neither Nick nor we particularly care for, such as Widmerpool, Pamela, Sillery, and Odo Stevens. Losing his friends has left a void in his life that will be very difficult to fill.

Nick's depression at the beginning of *Books Do Furnish a Room* affects us because it is so human and understandable. While we haven't all lost friends in war, we do know what it is like to have too much work to do, or worse, to have none at all. We understand how total and abrupt change can create a longing for our previous life. Nick's depression forces us to look more deeply into Nick's character, and to pray he finds solace somewhere.

©Nicholas Anschuetz, 2008

A PORTRAIT OF THE FLORES:
THE LOOK OF HIGH SOCIETY
CASSIDY CARPENTER

In *Books Do Furnish A Room* Nick Jenkins runs into Colonel Flores and his wife, the former Jean Templer, at a party at their house. The Flores' home in London is overflowing with flowers, ironic because of the meaning of their last name. It is also overflowing with alcohol. Both of these delights were particularly hard to obtain in post-war England. The decadence at the party is an overt reference to the wealth in the hands of this South American couple. Nick's comments about the Flores' dress, especially that of Jean's, gives an accurate timeline at which to set the party in *Dance* and reinforces their unbridled wealth. Hilary Spurling, the author of *Invitation to the Dance*, and Anthony Powell agreed that this party had taken place in the spring of 1946. This may be true as far as other details in the book are concerned, but based on the release of Dior's New Look – which Jean is wearing – the party would have to have taken place in the spring of 1947 instead.

Upon setting his eyes on Jean, Nick notices that she looked "rather superb in what was called 'The New Look.'" This look that Nick has picked up on is from the 1947 spring/summer collection by Christian Dior. This is first collection released by Dior, which founded its haute couture fashion house the year previous (*Metropolitan*). "Featuring rounded shoulders, a cinched waist, and very full skirt, the New Look celebrated ultra-femininity and opulence in women's fashion. After years of military and civilian uniforms, sartorial restrictions and shortages, Dior offered not merely a new look but a new outlook" (*Metropolitan*). Jean's appearance embodied this swift transition into an era of luxury. An example of the sort of dress Jean would have worn at such an event – entitled "Chérie" – can be seen in the collection of the Metropolitan Museum of Art (*Metropolitan*).

This sapphire blue dinner dress from the 1947 spring-summer collection is made of a changeant silk taffeta. It exemplifies the New Look in its "sloped shoulder, raised bust line, narrowed waist, and a monumental volume of skirt falling away from a padded hipline to below the calf" (*Christian Dior*). A dress as lavish as this would cost an obscene amount of money. Nick believes that Jean becoming "so fashionable had to be attributed, one supposed, to her husband" (95). A husband in such high society with equally high a pay roll would be needed to support fashions such as these.

Nick marvels at Jean's stark transition: "in the old days much of her charm -- so it had seemed -- had been to look like a well-turned-out school girl, rather than an enchantress on the cover of a fashion magazine." He now notices that she has a very slight foreign intonation in her speech, which complements her new haute couture look. The ease at which Jean has transitioned into her role as Madame Flores is not surprising in the least. Upon arrival at the party it becomes apparent to Nick that, "money was after all what Jean really liked. In fact Duport, even apart from his other failings, had not really been rich enough. It looked as if that problem were now resolved, Jean married to a rich man" (95).

The wealthy new addition to Jean's life is Colonel Carlos Flores, to Nick, the epitome of romanticism and prosperity. "Flores did posses the distinct look of Rudolph Valentino" (96). Valentino was a silent film star known as a sex and fashion idol (Rudolph Valentino): "Handsome, spruce and genial, the Colonel's English was almost more fluent than his wife's, at least in the sense that his language had that faintly old-world tinge that one associated with someone like Alfred Tolland" (96). The same romanticized, larger-than life perception is brought out in the description of the Colonel as resembling Valentino. The Flores' high society demeanor sets them distinctly on a higher plane than Nick.

The fashion adorning Colonel and Mrs. Flores boasts their high society profile and money that pays for it. Spurling identifies the Flores's party as happening in "early spring of 1946 (326)". The time at which Christian Dior released his New Look on to the fashion scene helps point out a possible mistake in the timeline of *Dance* – one that Powell agreed to, as he consulted with Spurling on her *Invitation to the Dance*. Nick's seemingly passive descriptions give us new insight into the lives of high society London.

Sources:

Christian Dior. Martin, Richard and Harold Koda. The Metropolitan Museum of Art: New York, 1997.
The Metropolitan Museum of Art. http://www.metmuseum.org/TOAH/HD/dior/ho_C.I.48.13a,b.htm. 22 Apr 2008.
The Rudolph Valentino Homepage. http://www.rudolph-valentino.com/ 22 Apr 2008.
Hilary Spurling. *Invitation to the Dance.* Little, Brown: Boston, 1978.
The World Almanac. http://www.worldalmanac.com/newsletter/en00038.jpg. 22 Apr 2008.

FUNERALS CAN BE FUNNY
WILL STORY

Usually in a book when a chapter is focused on a funeral that chapter tends to be sad. Chapter Two in *Books Do Furnish A Room* is set around Erridge's funeral. This doesn't discourage Powell from throwing humor into this chapter. In fact this chapter is one of the funniest chapters found in all of *Dance*. Powell fills this chapter with humor, keeping the reader laughing all the way through Erridge's funeral.

Widmerpool's party draws a lot of attention as it enters the church for Erridge's funeral. He is shown as the leader of this group as they find their seats. He "shot out the hand of a policeman directing traffic, to indicate where each was to sit of the group apparently under his command" (47). The image of Widmerpool acting as a policeman is easy for a reader of *Dance* to see, especially after his behavior in the military. If he were indeed a policeman, his uniform would no doubt be too small, just as his military one was. Pamela tests Widmerpool's power when she doesn't act exactly as he wishes, but he lets her insubordination pass.

Powell further lightens up this chapter with Pamela's sickness. She feels faint during the service and afterwards during the reception decides to leave early. While Nick escorts her to her car, she turns green and he recognizes that she is going to vomit. He asks her if she wants to go back "to the bathroom" (82), but it is too late. Pamela looks around the room and sees, "two tall oriental vessels ... standing five foot high.... [then] Pamela came to a decision. Moving rapidly forward... she turned away and leant forward. All was over in a matter of seconds" (82). Pamela vomits in one of the antique oriental vessels.

Widmerpool, Alfred Tolland, Quiggin, Craggs, and Gypsy arrive right after Pamela's illness. Widmerpool admires the antique urn that has just been vomited into. Powell uses this scene for a few reasons. He may want to suggest that Pamela might be pregnant, and that is why she is vomiting – though there is no mention of this possibility. He certainly makes Widmerpool look like a buffoon for liking the antique that has just been defaced. Finally this scene adds further macabre humor to the chapter.

Finally Powell describes the process of cleaning the antique vessel in one humorous paragraph. The action is undertaken by Nick, Jeavons, Hugo, "with shrewd advice from Roddy Cutts" (86). The reader is given a description of the four-man team struggling with this large object that seems never have been made to be cleaned anyway. Nick says, "The job took quite a long time. More than once the vase was nearly broken. We returned to the sitting-room with a good deal of relief that the business was at an end" (86). Powell uses this scene purely for comedic purposes. The image of Nick, Jeavons, and Hugo juggling this large vessel in a bathroom makes the reader laugh out loud.

Chapter Two of *Books Do Furnish a Room* is a great example of the humor that Powell uses throughout *Dance*. Even though the book is centered on a funeral, it is one of the funniest chapters to be found in the sequence. Its ending puts the lid on the humor with Dickie Umfraville revealing one of the funniest names for an alcoholic cocktail: "Death Comes for the Archbishop" (92).

©William Story, 2002

Widmerpool's Private Eye: The Untold Story
(In the Style of Julian Maclaren-Ross)
Alex Svec

The name's Quickshot, Buddy Quickshot, at least that's what I tell my clients. I'm a private eye. I'm known for two things, the way I handle my cases, and the way I handle my drink. It was dark, cold, rainy night when he came in. I was in deep conversation with a close friend of mine, my hipflask, and was about to strike up another one with the bottle of bourbon I keep in my bottom drawer. He was a sorry bloke, soaked through and rather clumsy. For whatever reason he seemed to hold himself quite high. I was planning on taking the night off, but then again, business wasn't as good as it had always been, and I had nasty relationship with a couple loan sharks. He claimed to have woman problems, who doesn't? He told me he suspected his wife was cheating on him; I didn't bother to ask why.

I headed out into the dark underbelly of London armed with a cigarette, my cosh, and a description of the broad I was supposed to follow. Pretty soon I realized I needed two things, a lead, and a drink. I knew where to find one. An hour later I was back on the streets. I needed to start somewhere, so I paid a visit to an old friend of mine. She called herself Chastity. She wasn't the type of girl you brought home to mom. We had always had a good arrangement – I kept the wineglass full; she kept the bed warm. I went to her place hoping to shed some light on the situation. I left a few hours later with only my wallet lighter. No further along than I was six hours ago I decided to call it a night. I was almost back at my place when I got jumped. There were three of them. Good odds for me any day. I was handling things pretty well, until the fourth bloke came from behind – lights out.

I woke up the next morning in some back alley. I needed a drink – bad. I asked the guy lying next to me; no dice. Walking once again to my apartment, head feeling like it had a run in with the business end of a log splitter, I couldn't help but wonder if the mugging was coincidence or not. Maybe I gave Chastity a bit too much information, whatever the reason, someone wanted me out of the picture, and if I wasn't careful next time, there would be no next time. Instead of landing in my apartment, I found myself once again in my office. I went out back to the small firing range I have to squeeze off a few rounds. I took ten shots; six were lead, the other four – bourbon. There was too much running through my head. Who was this Widmerpool bloke anyway? How did he score a trophy wife? And who were the monkeys trying to rub me off? I went to the one place I knew where both information and drinks come cheap.

The seedy pub – both its name and its description – many of the patrons there would sell their own mothers if you were offering enough coin. I ordered a drink, "Death Comes for the Archbishop." It tasted like battery acid mixed with motor oil; I ordered two more. I was getting somewhere with one of the regulars, when she walked in. The sight of her hit me harder than the slug of a .45. There could no mistaking, Widmerpool's broad had just walked in the door – Pamela. I reminded myself to remain cool; I was no use if I blew my cover. Business first as they say, and if I had anything to say about it we'd be doing business back at my place all night long. She hung around a good two hours, teasing the bar staff before she finally took off, I made sure to keep a good distance between us. I'd caught a lucky break and I knew it, but I wasn't about to complain. After tailing her for twenty minutes she ended up at a residence I soon identified as X Trapnel's. Another case solved. The Widmerpool bloke came in the next day and paid up. With paper once again in my pocket I decided I'd earned a few nights off. Anyways, I needed a drink.

©Alexander Svec, 2008

CHAPTER 11:
TEMPORARY KINGS

Out of all its 400-plus personages, *Dance* offers us a handful of minor characters that absolutely dominate the stage, even after they have left it. Uncle Giles, appearing in six volumes; Mrs. Erdleigh, in four; Dr. Trelawney, in only one, believe it or not – these figures cast long shadows over the entire series. They can even, in our minds, affect the earlier books; Henry Harrington, the friend that first introduced me to *Dance* (and author of an early essay on *Dance*), asked me, after I had read the fourth volume, *At Lady Molly's*, how I liked Dr. Trelawney, who does not appear until the sixth. After I met the good doctor, I could see how Hank had inflated his role. Simply, Trelawney fills the (ball) room.

So does Pamela Widmerpool. She appears in only three volumes although after her last one we cannot picture Nick Jenkins's life without her in it. She dominates *Dance* and our imaginations as she grows from sulky bitchiness to straight-out madness. We watch her men – the long line in *The Military Philosophers* ending with Widmerpool, X. Trapnel in *Books Do Furnish a Room*, and Gwinnett in *Temporary Kings* – as they mostly grovel at her feet and occasionally die. She overwhelms them and us, until she reaches her apotheosis with Gwinnett.

Pamela overwhelmed the students as well. During our time with her three books, they wrote twelve essays about her, roughly one-fifth of both classes' output. For *Temporary Kings* I have included two of these – one about her similarities with Candaules' queen and the other about the irony of her as a "temporary queen" in a book full of temporary kings.

A number of other essay topics emerged from this volume. There were a number of factual research papers, Although their pieces are not included here, several students were interested in writing about Cold War espionage, comparing Widmerpool and Dr. Belkin with their real-life counterparts: Burgess, MacLean, *et al.* An interesting paper about the canals of Venice, their geography and history – and how they influence the novel – does appear.

Finally as we got closer to the end of *Dance*, the opportunity for retrospective assessments of themes and characters arose. Jimmy Yang produced an example of this: a thoughtful piece on Mrs. Erdleigh's predictions, and how they play out over the entire series. Jimmy's paper showed an unexpected benefit from the internet publication of the entire course: he was able to cite another student's paper – in this case, Cassidy Carpenter's observation about Powell and Nick sharing the same birthday. It was satisfying indeed to see that all the work we had done earlier in the year remained to support us now as we brought the series to conclusion.

SYNOPSIS

Temporary Kings begins in Venice in the summer of 1958. Jenkins is attending a literary conference organized by Mark Members. There he meets a don, Dr. Emily Brightman, and Russell Gwinnett, an American who plans to write a biography of X. Trapnel. The French writer, Ferrand-Seneschal, who was to have attended the conference, has died in a London hotel room; they learn that Pamela Widmerpool may have been present at his death. Jenkins recalls the death of X. Trapnel, some ten years earlier. Widmerpool has lost his seat in Parliament, but has been made a Life Peer. Dr. Brightman reveals Pamela is presently in Venice. Jenkins recalls his father's old one-time friend Dan Tokenhouse, with whom Jenkins worked publishing art books, who lives in Venice.

Jenkins, Gwinnett, and Dr. Brightman visit the Bragadin palace, where they can see the ceiling painting by Tiepolo, a mythological scene of a king (Candaules), queen, and voyeuristic general (Gyges). Present are Pamela Widmerpool and Louis Glober, whom Jenkins recalls from a dinner years ago in England. Pamela and Glober appear to be having some kind of affair. Gwinnett tries to extract some information about Trapnel from Pamela, and Widmerpool arrives, noticeably disturbed about the absence of one of the conference delegates, a "Dr. Belkin."

Tokenhouse and Jenkins meet to discuss art and encounter Ada and Glober. They all go to see Tokenhouse's paintings. Widmerpool arrives, looking for Belkin – who may be a Communist – and Glober buys a painting. Later Ada explains that Pamela wants a role in Glober's film. Gwinnett and Pamela meet at the Basilica, where she grabs him inappropriately. Rosie and Odo Stevens meet Jenkins and Gwinnett. Gwinnett gives Trapnel's Commonplace Book to Jenkins for safekeeping.

Jenkins goes to Bagshaw's house and hears of Pamela's naked escapade when Gwinnett was staying with him. Jenkins attends a military reunion, where he sees Cheesman, who tells him of

Stringham's death in the POW camp. Sunny Farebrother explains that Widmerpool may be tried for espionage.

A music party is held at Rosie and Odo Stevens's house. Moreland, Audrey Maclintick, Glober, Polly Duport, the Widmerpools, Jimmy Stripling and Mrs. Erdleigh all attend. At the end Moreland becomes ill. As everyone is leaving, Mrs. Erdleigh predicts her own death and tells Pamela to take care. Pamela makes a scene by revealing Glober's sexual habits to Polly and Widmerpool's voyeurism with her and Ferrand-Seneschal to everyone else. Widmerpool insults Glober, who punches him. Pamela disappears.

Jenkins receives a letter from Gwinnett, discussing Pamela and X. Trapnel, and Glober's death. He then flashes back to one of his final conversations with Moreland, in which the Gyges-Candaules myth, Sir Magnus Donners, and Pamela's mysterious death are major topics. At the very end of the book, Jenkins meets a despairing Widmerpool, on his way to the House of Lords.

CHARACTER LIST

The major characters in this volume, arranged by chapter:

Chapter 1

Mark Members – organizer of literary conference in Venice
Dr. Emily Brightman – a scholar, don at a woman's college
Russell Gwinnett - an American scholar, interested in X. Trapnel

Chapter 2

Jacky Bragadin - rich American living in Venice
Baby Wentworth Clarini – wife of an Italian filmmaker
Louis Glober – rich American playboy, movie director
Pamela Flitton Widmerpool – the worst person ever (Doug Presley)
Kenneth Widmerpool – now a Life Peer

Chapter 3

Dan Tokenhouse – old friend of Jenkins's, amateur socialist artist in Venice
Ada Leintwardine – novelist, married to J.G. Quiggin
Rosie Manasch Stevens – supporter of the arts
Odo Stevens – her husband

Chapter 4

Lindsey Bagshaw - now a TV personality
Avril, Felicity, Stella - stepdaughters of Bagshaw
Sunny Farebrother - old friend of Jenkins
Cheesman - Stringham's commander from WWII

Chapter 5

Polly Duport – Jean Templer and Bob Duport's daughter, an actress

Hugh Moreland – composer, Jenkins's best friend

Audrey Maclintick – woman living with Moreland

Mrs. Myra Erdleigh – an eccentric fortune-teller

Jimmy Stripling – an old car enthusiast, involved with Mrs. Erdleigh

PAMELA WIDMERPOOL: MODEL FOR TIEPOLO
DANA FEENY

Powell links Pamela to Tiepolo's work throughout his description of the ceiling fresco in *Temporary Kings*. He suggests that she could have been a part of the painting, relating her to the naked woman in its center. Pamela's interest in it draws everyone's attention upwards and sparks a conversation that both describes and analyzes it. I believe this painting is an insight into her personality and the description and discussion about it applies to her as well this fictional work by Tiepolo.

"Pamela's own tints hinted that she herself, only a moment before, had floated down out of those cloudy vertical perspectives, perhaps compelled to do so by the artist himself, displeased that her crimson and peacock shades struck too extravagant a note, one that disturbed rather than enriched a composition, which, for all its splendor, remained somehow tenebrous too" (82). The description of this painting begins with that description. Powell has intentionally described Pamela in terms of the painting, and the painting in terms of Pamela. Clearly they are not one and the same, but this depiction allows us imaginatively to place Pamela in the picture. It lets us know that this is about her. It gives a sense of foreshadowing to the ceiling painting. More than just a painting, it is connected, some mysterious way, to Pamela Widmerpool.

"The lady, less intent on making love, anxious to augment pending pleasure by delicious delay, somehow remembering her own neglect of some desirable adjunct, or necessary precaution, incident on what was about to take place, had paused" (84). In context, this sentence clearly describes the woman in the center of the painting, but when isolated it could be a camouflaged analysis of Pamela. The phrases "augment pending pleasure" and "delicious delay" fit right in with her selfish, manipulative tendencies. Her sexual promiscuity is not just about her loving sex, but also about her loving control and her loving to create the downfall of others.

She augments her own pleasure by manipulating people with sex, but also by continuously surprising others with her harmful, unjustified, and often-unprovoked actions, for example when she threw X Trapnel's manuscript into the Maida Vale canal.

Powell himself relates Pamela to the woman in the painting when he presents the possibility that, "like Pamela herself --- she was frigid but wanted a lot of it all the same" (84). Nick makes this remark as a possible explanation for the body language of the hesitating queen painted on the ceiling. As the myth goes, she has paused not because of her Pamela-like frigid desires, but because she is distracted by the man hiding in the corner. Regardless, this clear association of her with the queen is not to be ignored. The intimate situation of nudity, the two men, and the focus on the undecided naked woman creates a scenario of vulnerability, hesitation, and manipulation that hits close to Pamela.

> One of the paradoxes about Pamela was a sexuality, in one sense almost laughably ostentatious, the first thing you noticed about her; in another, something equally connected with sex that seemed reluctant, extorted, a possession she herself utterly refused to share with anyone. (81)

She is an anomaly that we cannot fully understand, but throughout the analysis of Tiepolo's ceiling painting, Powell brings forth just a few sides of the polygon that is Pamela Widmerpool.

©Dana Feeny, 2008

TEMPORARY QUEEN: THE IRONY OF PAMELA'S DEATH
JAY PARK

As Pamela stares at the fresco of Candaules and Gyges, she asks, "Who is the naked man with the stand?" (83) Only referencing the sensuality of the scene, Pamela casually ignores Brightman and Glober as they carefully delineate the myth of the King of Lydia, Candaules, and his guard, Gyges. More importantly, however, Pamela fails to recognize the recurring theme of the temporary kings, as she focuses only on the intent of King Candaules – not the end result. Throughout *A Dance to the Music of Time*, Pamela has represented the Queen figure – upholding her position while her suitors rotated just as temporary kings; however, the penultimate book, *Temporary Kings*, represents a reversal of roles, as Pamela ironically plays the role of Gwinnett's temporary queen.

From her relationships with X Trapnel, Ferrand-Seneschal, and Widmerpool, Powell has almost overemphasized the allure and danger of Lady Widmerpool. As one who only expressed "emotional warmth ... towards the dead" (102), Pamela proves to be a threat once again in *Temporary Kings*, particularly to the next potential King Candaules, Gwinnett, an American scholar writing a biography of our beloved X. Trapnel. However, from his initial description, Powell hints that Gwinnett may be quite different from Pamela's other suitors, some of them by now deceased.

More than aware of Pamela's acid personality, even Nick is hesitant to introduce Gwinnett to Pamela, as he contemplates "the question of whether or not to introduce [him] ... without saying some preliminary word first" (99). However, his fear of a potential scene between Pamela and Gwinnett is suddenly quelled as he realizes that the American scholar is quite different from her previous suitors. "The mere fact that Gwinnett himself, not Pamela, took the offensive"(100), makes quite an impression on Jenkins. Having watched so many of Pamela's kings – from Peter

Templar to X Trapnel – Nick goes on to parallel "Gwinnett's tone with Pamela" as he "[conveyed] only the merest atom of overt friendliness" (101). As Gwinnett does not seem the least bit overwhelmed by Pamela's sheer sexual appeal, it becomes quite clear that this temporary king might not be quite so temporary.

Continuing to question Pamela about X Trapnel, Gwinnett continues to reveal his immense ability to match Pamela's previously unparalleled aggression. For instance, in response to her threat to destroy Trapnel's Commonplace Book – which contained portions of the brilliant but destroyed manuscript *Profiles in String* – Gwinnett bluntly responds, "I entirely believe you, Lady Widmerpool, but you don't have the Commonplace Book" (173). Furious because of his nonchalance, Pamela throws the crocodile shoulder bag given to her by Glober over the side of the bridge to imitate Trapnel's "necessary sacrifice" of his swordstick. Immune to her tactics, however, Gwinnett "stood there openly unimpressed" (173) by her open aggression. In essence, despite her irrational actions, Pamela cannot seem to control Gwinnett, as she has done so many others. Almost uninterested in her for reasons other than her knowledge of X Trapnel, the American scholar establishes his dominance over her. Nick asks himself, "Would Gwinnett be able to give her Death?" (102), in the sense that Pamela might add Gwinnett to her collection of dead suitors; however, as the relationship develops, this inquiry seems to be entirely ironic because Pamela will most certainly not obtain any sort of physical or emotional Death from Gwinnett. It will be just the other way around.

In a twisted series of events, Pamela Widmerpool commits suicide to satisfy Gwinnett's necrophiliac tendencies – which Powell gently hints at prior to her death. In an entirely ironic series of events, Pamela's death comes full circle. Her own need for dominance causes her to desire Gwinnett – who for the most part seems uninterested – to reach an irrational level, so irrational in fact that she commits suicide in her last attempt to satisfy his pleasures. Although Powell leads the reader to believe that Pamela will add Gwinnett to her list of Temporary Kings, it is in fact the Queen who is added to the growing list of the deceased.

The Canals of Venice
James Seman

The city of Venice is famous for its distinctive canals. In fact, these canals were so distinctive and impressive that Tsar Peter the Great of the Russian Empire copied them in an effort to make his capital seem more impressive. In the penultimate book of Anthony Powell's *Dance to the Music of Time*, *Temporary Kings*, Nick Jenkins attends a conference of writers in Venice. During his time there, Nick is surrounded by the history and culture of this venerable city.

The city of Venice is built on an archipelago of 118 islands formed by approximately 150 canals. The canals are bridged by about 400 bridges, which are the only land routes to the different islands of the archipelago. In part because of the difficulty that lies in navigating this city of bridges, there are no cars in Venice. In fact, it is unique among European cities in that it remains a functioning city in the 21st century without any cars or trucks. Instead, walking or boats remain as the dominant forms of transportation around the city of Venice.

The best-known example of transport is the famous Venetian gondola. For many years, gondolas were the chief method of transportation within the city of Venice itself. The traditional black color of the gondola dates back from a sumptuary law, but they are still painted black today because of tradition. Tourists now constitute the primary customers of these vessels, although Venetians use them for traditional reasons like weddings and funerals. Motorized ferries, traghetti, have mostly supplanted gondolas in their role as the chief mode of transport in the city of Venice itself.

Over the course of Nick's conference in Venice, he meets Russell Gwinnett, who is writing a book on X. Trapnel, and wants to meet Pamela. When he finally does so, he encounters her in the Basilica di San Marco a Venezia, Saint Mark's Basilica. The Basilica, built to honor St. Mark, is extremely ornate on both the inside and outside. There is some irony in Mark's cathedral being in Venice. If one tenth of Godly behavior is "thou shalt not steal," San Marco should be elsewhere; his remains were stolen by Venetian merchants in the mid 800s, and were later housed in a temporary church on the same spot as the present Basilica. In this very Basilica Pamela steals Gwinnett's heart, by grabbing his attention and his other parts as well. This action sets up both of their demises, as she later commits suicide so he can enjoy having sex with her corpse, and he, as a result of her death, abandons academia to become a water-skiing instructor in Spain.

The background of Venice plays a part in shaping the rest of *Temporary Kings*. By using Venice, once the most powerful and decadent of all the Italian city-states, Anthony Powell shows just how important the events of this novel are. Although most of the characters are getting older and past the prime of their lives, they are still capable of making decisions that have a huge impact on other characters' lives. Pamela dies, but not before revealing some of Widmerpool's dirty secrets, which sets the stage for his downfall. Likewise, Gwinnett is no longer a literary figure, so this event that leads to Pamela's death leads also to his own literary death. This death, combined with that of Pamela, sets the tone for the rest of the novel and the rest of the series. As time marches on, more and more of Nick's old friends will die too.

Sources:

1. "Venice." Wikipedia. http://en.wikipedia.org/wiki/Venice. 20 May 2008. 22 May 2008.
2. "Gondola." Wikipedia. http://en.wikipedia.org/wiki/ Gondola. 24 May 2008

Mrs. Erdleigh's Prognostications
Jimmy Yang

Prognostications have been an integral part of *A Dance to the Music of Time* since the very beginning. One that has stuck in our minds from the very beginning was Stringham's prediction that Widmerpool "would be the death of [him]." (*QU* 49) We have read long enough by now to know how accurate Stringham was. It is therefore self-evident that Myra Erdleigh, a woman who makes her living making predictions about people's lives, would be significant throughout the story. Though she was introduced seemingly as a character unrelated to the story at the beginning of *The Acceptance World*, she has given us critical information about the future of various characters as the story advanced.

Myra Erdleigh was first introduced in the Ufford, the hotel Uncle Giles used to frequent, at the beginning of *The Acceptance World*. At that time through a brief exchange about astrological signs, we were given enough information to deduce that Nick's birthday coincides with Powell's, certainly a fitting introduction to the character of Mrs. Erdleigh. * She then went on to predict that Nick would have an affair with Jean, and that another man would appear in their relationship. When we finish the book, we assume that this man is Jimmy Stripling; however, we discover several books later, in *The Valley of Bones* that Jimmy Brent was also involved with Jean at the time, and perhaps Mrs. Erdleigh's prognostication referred to him.

Mrs. Erdleigh makes her most crucial predictions when in *The Military Philosophers* she meets Pamela Widmerpool (then Pamela Flitton) for the first time. This moment occurs during the war, and her revelations about Pamela Widmerpool are significant. Nick, Pamela, and Odo Stevens find her during an air raid in the apartment complex where Nick lives. When Odo asks Mrs. Erdleigh to "tell Pam's fortune," (*MP* 133) she gives us another premonition, as in *The Acceptance World*. She tells us that "death ... surrounds [Pamela's] nativity" (*MP* 132), which we take as a connection to her uncanny ability to get her lovers (in particular Peter Templer) killed. Furthermore, Mrs. Erdleigh says that Pamela is "not always well governed in [herself]" and that she is prone to "*la débauche, l'effronterie, la licence ...*" (*MP* 135). In *Temporary Kings*, we see both of these prognostications fulfilled in surprising truth. Pamela herself admits that she was in bed with Ferrand-Seneschal: "You don't have to be told Leon-Joseph croaked in bed with me" (261).

Mrs. Erdleigh's most recent entry is in this very book. In *Temporary Kings*, she makes new predictions about Pamela. She appears again only at the end of the book, but as before, her predictions will undoubtedly be significant. "My dear, beware. You are near the abyss. You stand at its utmost edge. Do not forget the warning I gave you when you showed me your palm on that dread night" (260). Something big is going to happen to Pamela Widmerpool. Mrs. Erdleigh knows it, and it is shown to us by the dramatic exchange following Mrs. Erdleigh's warning.

Pamela Widmerpool is not likely to be a character in the story for much longer. It seems that everything has been going wrong for her. She has found a man she could not break, Russell Gwinnett, and she seems to have gone mad. Her relationship with her husband is breaking down, and despite his usual resilience in the face of her actions, even he has resorted to violence against her. Mrs. Erdleigh's warning to her can be taken in more than a figurative sense – that in taking the plunge into the abyss, her life will come to an end. Then, on page 269, we learn that it has.

Mrs. Erdleigh has not been the most visible character in *A Dance to the Music of Time*. Gliding in and out of the story like a ghost, she nevertheless maintains a solid grasp on the plot's movement. Although she does not have a direct impact on it, she is omniscient, watching and prophesizing as the action unfolds. Her most important predictions are directed toward Pamela Widmerpool, undoubtedly one of the most unpredictable characters that we meet, who destroys men all around the world. But Mrs. Erdleigh sees right through her, and just as with anyone else, she makes crucial predictions about her future.

---

* This observation was made by Cassidy Carpenter, in her paper, "It's All in the Cards: Cartomancy in *A Dance to the Music of Time,*" in Chapter 2, *The Acceptance World*, in this collection.

CHAPTER 12:
HEARING SECRET HARMONIES

After promenading with my classes through *Dance* for nine months, I – and those students that had been in the class since September – had to undergo the wrenching separation of saying good-bye to the world we had been immersed in for so long. It was difficult for some of them, although given their position in life – i.e., just a few days from high school graduation – there were many other separations looming all around them. Leaving Powell's world was simply one more bittersweet departure, and by no means the most significant one they were facing.

Hearing Secret Harmonies was closest to them chronologically, and consequently its world was more familiar to them than those of the earlier books. Many of their parents grew up hearing about hippie cults and counter-cultural demonstrations, and films like *Easy Rider* and *Good Morning, Vietnam* are still enough a part of popular culture to provide them imaginative reference to the Harmony crew and the Quiggin twins. These characters seemed nasty enough to appeal to their eighteen-year-old taste for the grotesque. So I was a little surprised that only one essay treated the charismatic, unpleasant, grotesque Scorpio Murtlock. That one, by Becca Zinsmeister, turned out to be a perceptive piece that linked him, not with the mage Dr. Trelawney (a common enough comparison), but with Pamela Widmerpool. (Becca had written about Pamela before.)

I was glad that for this final book most of the students chose to look back over much or all of the series. I have chosen to include William Koven's interesting look back at Matilda, which he casts as the outline, or treatment, for a play. Seventy percent of the essays for *HSH* were retrospectives that focused on a single character. Five of these attempted a final assessment of Widmerpool. Who could be surprised at this? The students' initial response to the Frog Footman was sympathy, when he was ragged by the other boys at school. Later it shifted to amusement, distaste, frank dislike, and finally something akin to pity. Naturally, they wanted to make sense out of such a broad range of responses.

There were two students that wrote about their personal experience in reading the entire sequence. Corey Simpson is a witty, intelligent writer, and her paper shows that all of us with poor memories are at an advantage: we can reread books we know we have loved but can't exactly recall why with more pleasure than those who can remember everything. And Madeleine Fawcett has written a wonderful explanation of how *Dance* has provided all of us a template to live and understand our own lives. As she writes in her conclusion, "My dance continues ..."

Synopsis

Hearing Secret Harmonies begins at Jenkins's house in the country in 1968. Jenkins and Isobel take Scorpio Murtlock, Barnabas Henderson, Fiona Cutts, and Rusty - who are camping on their land in a horse-drawn caravan - fishing for crayfish. Returning, they meet Mr. Gauntlett, who is looking for his bitch, Daisy. Murtlock tells him where to find her, then instructs his followers in what rites to follow with the crayfish. They leave the next morning.

Jenkins muses about Ariosto's *Orlando Furioso* and the Valley of Lost Things. He and Isobel watch a St. John Clarke special on TV, later a news report of Widmerpool being attacked by the Quiggin twins, who throw paint over him. The Donners-Brebner Prize Committee - Jenkins, Members, Dr. Brightman, advised by Delavacquerie - agree to award the prize to Russell Gwinnett for his biography of X. Trapnel, discussing Widmerpool's possible objections. Jenkins meet Farebrother coming from Jimmy Stripling's funeral.

The literary crowd assembles for the Prize dinner. Gwinnett appears, looking like Trapnel's death-head swordstick with his bald scalp. Widmerpool arrives with the Quiggin twins, much disconcerting their parents. He gives a radical speech, embracing the counter-culture, and the twins set off firecrackers and a stink bomb. Widmerpool arranges to meet with Gwinnett, who is unaffected by the disturbances.

Jenkins attends a Royal Academy dinner, meeting Canon Fenneau, who knew Dr. Trelawney and who has known Murtlock since he was a child. Widmerpool approaches them, asking Fenneau to introduce him to Murtlock. Fenneau warns him against this idea. Afterwards, the canon reveals that Murtlock wants to meet Widmerpool.

Jenkins learns that Widmerpool has joined forces with Murtlock. Delavacquerie, involved with Polly Duport, tells him that Col. Flores, Jean Templer Duport's most recent husband, has been assassinated, mentioning also that Gwinnett is investigating the Murtlock/Widmerpool cult. A group of local preservationists meet by Devil's Fingers, a stone-age monument in Jenkins's neighborhood. Mr. Gauntlett tells of a neighbor's report of strange doings at the Fingers the night before. Jenkins discovers Gwinnett walking nearby, having been up all night at these rites, which were violent. Later Delavacquerie tells Jenkins that he has broken off things with Polly. He has provided Murtlock with Gwinnett's address in exchange for Fiona Cutts's release from the cult. She now lives at his flat.

At Stourwater, the Jenkinses attend the marriage of Fiona's brother Sebastian Cutts to Clare Akworth, granddaughter of Sir Bertram. Fiona and Gwinnett, who have married the day before, now turn up at the reception. The Harmony crowd – Widmerpool, Henderson, Bithel, and others – appear. Chuck, Henderson's old boyfriend, is at the wedding, and convinces Henderson to leave the cult to come with him. Widmerpool, now visibly unstable, abases himself before Sir Bertram, because years ago he got Sir Bertram kicked out of school for having written a love note to Peter Templer. Flavia Wisebite is enraged at Widmerpool's presence and collapses on him. Bithel gets drunk. Murtlock, showing up, allows Henderson to leave the cult, refuses to allow Widmerpool to leave also, and takes Bithel home.

While burning trash, Jenkins flashes back to a visit to Henderson's art gallery to see the Deacon Centennial exhibit, where Bob Duport, Jean, and Polly are present. Polly says she is marrying Delavacquerie. After they leave, as Jenkins discusses the Murtlock cult with Henderson, Bithel arrives in a dreadful state, with the Modigliani drawing once owned by Charles Stringham, passed now to Widmerpool from Pamela. Widmerpool has died while running half naked through the woods. Back at his trash-burning, Jenkins meditates on a passage by Burton, and the *Dance* comes to an end.

CHARACTER LIST

The major characters in this volume, arranged by chapter:

Chapter 1

Isobel – Jenkins's wife
Fiona Cutts – Isobel's niece
Scorpio Murtlock – "Harmony" cult leader
Barnabas Henderson – cult follower
Rusty – female cult follower
Mr. Gauntlett – a farmer, neighbor of Jenkins

Chapter 2

J.G. Quiggin – publisher
Ada Leintwardine – novelist, married to J.G. Quiggin
Amanda, Belinda – their twin daughters
Mark Members – poet, member of Donners Prize Committee
Dr. Emily Brightman – scholar, member of Donners Prize Committee
L. O. Salvidge – critic
"Ken" Widmerpool – Life Peer, now chancellor of a university
Matilda Donners – widow of Sir Magnus
Gibson Delavacquerie – P.R. man for Donners-Brebner
Sunny Farebrother – old acquaintance of Jenkins

Chapter 3

Russell Gwinnett – an American scholar, biographer of X. Trapnel

Chapter 4

Rev. Canon Paul Fenneau – a cleric, first met as undergrad in QU

Chapter 5

Roddy and Susan Cutts - Fiona's parents
Sir Bertram Akworth - grandfather of Clare, the bride
Chuck - former boyfriend of Barnabas
Bithel - old army colleague of Jenkins
Flavia Wisebite – Stringham's sister and Widmerpool's mother-in-law

Chapter 6

Jean Templer Duport Flores – old heartthrob of Jenkins
Bob Duport – Jean's ex-husband
Polly Duport – Jean and Bob's daughter, an actress

Scorp and Pam
Becca Zinsmeister

In *Hearing Secret Harmonies* Powell introduces Scorpio Murtlock, a young man with a dominating personality. Murtlock's character is very reminiscent of the notorious Pamela Widmerpool. Outwardly both are known for their beauty. Pamela attracts men wherever she goes. Hardly anyone is able to resist her and those that she ensnares rarely walk away from the encounter unscathed. Paul Fenneau describes Murtlock as "a beautiful boy" to Nick (129). Murtlock's ability to attract others is further confirmed by Henderson who states he believed everyone to be "in love with Scorp," just as he was (261).

The similarities, however, do not stop at the their handsome features. Both Pamela and Murtlock share similar personalities and behavioral traits. The most apparent mutual characteristic is their ability to dominate other people completely. Pamela's wake, washing over both men and women, is not merely destructive but deadly. Most recently we have looked on as she ruins X. Trapnel by destroying both his beloved manuscript and his spirit – and ultimately, his life. Nick remarks, "Now, it had become Trapnel's turn to join the dynasty of Pamela's dead lovers" (102 *TK*). Her ability to dominate men is best exemplified in her relationship with Widmerpool, for after numerous affairs and purposeful embarrassments on her part, he remains married to her until her death.

Powell does not present the reader with such a detailed history of Murtlock's victims. Fenneau vaguely tells Nick of the choirmaster that Murtlock developed an "unhappy influence over" and how Murtlock destroyed the man's reputation and cost him his job (132). Murtlock also exhibits complete power over his cult. His control over Widmerpool is astounding, as he forces him to do penance for past misdeeds and starkly refuses to allow him to leave, which eventually leads to his death. Even those like Henderson and Fiona, who have left the cult, haven't quite escaped his thrall. Henderson jumps at the chance to hear when he believes that Nick has news about Murtlock and Fiona appears frightened when she encounters Murtlock at the wedding, literally reaching out to Gwinnett for support.

The pursuit of Gwinnett is another thing that Pamela and Murtlock share. Gwinnett is the first male that Pamela has actively chased after and one of the few who seems immune to her sinister nature. In fact Gwinnett appears to have gotten two things that he wanted from Pamela, as Powell hints towards the reasons behind Pamela's suicide. Normally, men involved with Pamela are completely destroyed; however Gwinnett survives and goes on to write an award-winning biography. Murtlock also hunts down Gwinnett, sending Fiona to Delavacquerie several times in order to get in touch with him. After the ritual at the Devil's Fingers, he tells Nick how Murtlock wanted him to be "present at the rites that they were planning" (166). Much as he was with Pamela, Gwinnett is able to resist Murtlock and does not feel the need to submit to his way of life – although resisting Scorp is physically more difficult than resisting Pam. Ironically, after meeting Murtlock, Gwinnett gets married, something that the cult preaches against.

Several scenes in which Powell depicts Murtlock are remarkably similar to ones previously displaying Pamela. For example, when Murtlock addresses his followers at the wedding he begins with a light, albeit "sneering bantering manner" before becoming "consumed with cold rage," reminding everyone, especially Widmerpool, that he is in charge (237). In *Temporary Kings* Pamela adopts the same method at the Steven's party as she enters into conversation with Polly Duport while waiting for her ride. She begins with a "gentle" almost "shy" tone as though trying to lure those around her into a false sense of security. (256 *TK*) Then suddenly the situation becomes "highly charged" and Pamela's quiet inquiries turn malicious (257 *TK*). The parallels between Pamela and Murtlock grow in number as the events in *Hearing Secret Harmonies* unfold. After Pamela's death Powell appears to have resurrected her spirit and placed it into Scorpio Murtlock.

©Rebecca Zinsmeister, 2008

Matilda's Story: A Play
William Koven

A Dance to the Music of Time treats many different themes throughout the various novels. In particular, Powell gives attention to different forms of art including painting, music, and writing. One form of art that Powell seems to pay less explicit attention to, at least in the latter eight novels I am more familiar with, is theater. Rather than raising the subject of theater in one particular novel or set of novels, I think that Powell treats theater over the course of many books through one of my favorite characters, Matilda. In particular I think that Matilda's story throughout *Dance* reads much like the outline of a play. Since I particularly enjoy theater and playwriting, I find Matilda's story fascinating.

The Given Circumstances
    We find out that before Matilda first appears in *A Dance to the Music of Time*, she was once called Betty Updike, was briefly married to Carolo, and was one of Sir Magnus Donners's girls for a period of time. Then, her story opens when she performs with Norman Chandler in *The Duchess of Malfi*.

--- **Act I** ---

Scene I:
(*enter Moreland*)
    At first, Matilda's story is intertwined with Moreland's. He first introduces Matilda, an actress, to Nick when he brings him to see *The Duchess of Malfi*. Afterwards, they go backstage where they meet Matilda and Norman. "Matilda Wilson jumped up from her stool as soon as she saw Moreland. Throwing her arms around his neck, she kissed him on the nose" (*CCR* 46). Like the beginning of any good play, we immediately know what the characters want. Moreland and Matilda are in love.

Scene II:

Matilda is now married to Moreland and things seem to be going well. "In the earlier stages of marriage, Matilda was keeping pace pretty well with circumstances not always easy from shortage of money" (*CCR* 98). Then it happens: Matilda is pregnant. The first major obstacle is reached, and just as it should, the stakes of Matilda and Moreland's marriage are raised. But right at the end of the scene tragedy strikes; Matilda has a miscarriage. Such tragedy now gives us a chance to really get a feel for the characters, since character can be described as how a person reacts to a situation under pressure.

Scene III:

Moreland has somehow finished his symphony and Mrs. Fox throws a party for him. It is at this party we discover that perhaps Moreland is not as strong a character as we might have hoped. He is having an affair with Pricilla Tolland. Matilda knows of the affair. She is torn up about it and is unsure what she should do. Once again, another obstacle is reached and we are given a chance to see more of Matilda's character. She sticks it out. She knows that Moreland will come back to her. Indeed, after the death of his friend Maclintick, Moreland breaks off his love affair with Pricilla.

Scene IV:

(*enter Donners*)

Matilda and Moreland are now living in the country right near Stourwater, the castle of Sir Magnus Donners. On the surface it appears that their marriage is still going strong. Moreland, however, seems quite depressed and it is Matilda this time that has to deal with temptation. Along with Nick and Isobel, they spend an interesting dinner at Stourwater, which includes taking photographs of the party acting out the seven deadly sins. And then, at the end of the scene, the play reaches a form of climax: Matilda has had enough and leaves Moreland for Donners.

(*exit Moreland*)

Act II

Scene I:

A party. Matilda is doing well. She is seen now with Donners. Matilda seems quite happy in her new life, "To be rather older suited her; that or being married to a member of the Cabinet" (*MP* 207). And yet, despite her seeming happiness, she can't quite forget Moreland. "Obviously Matilda still took quite a keen interest in Moreland and his condition" (MP 208). The scene closes, once again, with the impression of Matilda being happy with her new position in life.

(*exit Donners*)

Scene II:

Much older now, Matilda has been widowed. For a short time after Donners's death she stays in the world of politics and high life, but then begins to let that slip, maintaining only a close circle of friends. In her widowhood she has a brief affair with Odo Stevens. But now she runs into yet another question: what should she do with herself in late life? In answer, she sets up the Donners literature award for biography. Yet years and years later, even after he is dead, Matilda just can't quite forget Moreland. "She had never been unwilling to speak of Moreland, often talking of their doings together," (59). Her long satisfying life lived out, she finally comes to a dramatic end befitting with her early career as an actress. Matilda simply tells a friend, Delavacquerie, that she won't be returning to London at the end of the summer.

End

Matilda's story in *A Dance to the Music of Time* makes a perfect outline for a very interesting play. I am quite tempted, given the opportunity, to actually try and write a play based on Matilda and Powell's other characters. Although Powell does not treat theater in the same way he treats painting, music, and writing, through both Matilda's doings and her personality he does give sense of the theater and theatrics.

Until the Next Dance: Why I'll Be Back
Corey Simpson

I am fortunate to possess one of the traits most desired by those who love to read; namely, I have the approximate memory retention of a goldfish. This did make my first reading of *Dance* rather difficult, especially considering Nick's fondness for reintroducing obscure minor characters we haven't seen in decades, but I also have the distinct advantage of being able to reread without growing bored.

I've never spent such a long time on one book. Usually I finish something in a day or two at most; this one, however, I've been working on since September. I've read it, I've dissected it, I've analyzed it, and I've listened to papers from my classmates on every possible topic connected with the story. It has become a constant in my life, on a level with other nice things like breathing. And, also like breathing, I can neither remember what it is like to exist without the *Dance* nor particularly want to find out.

Rereading it won't be quite the same, of course. Forgetful I may be, but I'll never again be able to read *A Question of Upbringing* and think that the rest of the series will focus on the friendship between Stringham, Templer, and Nick. I'll never be able to really pity Widmerpool again, though I did in the beginning. Knowing what I know now, I won't think that Nick's romance with Jean is quite so adorable. But I will know the characters and their quirks, and I will be as pleased to see them again as I would any other old friend.

To be sure, I'll need some time before I return. I'll need time to properly forget before I can take pleasure in remembering. Most importantly, I need to take a break, because at present I relate everything in my life to *Dance* and I think my friends will mutiny if I don't stop doing it soon. You know you've been reading too much of it if your own astrological sign now distresses you with its distasteful connections to the slimy Murtlock, if you can't think of the Seven Deadly Sins without a giggle, if you've made a mental note never to name any of your children "Pamela," or if your thoughts tend to run to page-long sentences of ridiculously elaborate prose. But these are minor concerns, and will no doubt fade with time. I find that I am far more worried about the implications of another *Dance* reflex I've developed recently, which threatens to become a permanent affliction. I am hesitant to disclose it because I have reason to believe it is contagious, but I think it better that you learn it from me than to realize it in horror while flipping through the radio stations. In short, my friends, this book has changed us, and you will remember it every time you hear the opening notes of the Def Leppard song "Pour Some Sugar On Me" and think instantly, automatically, of Widmerpool.

©Corey Simpson, 2008

Dancing Along
Madeleine Fawcett

The final pages of *A Dance to the Music of Time* have coincided with the "final pages" of my Andover career. It has been very interesting to follow the lives of Nick, Stringham, Templer, Widmerpool and many other fascinating characters on their journey through life, while simultaneously traveling along with my fellow classmates on a journey of our own. In "the longest novel ever written," which unfolds over several decades, Anthony Powell addresses death, reconnection, childhood, the arts, marriage, the "supernatural," adolescence, infidelity, childbearing, alcoholism, and other trials and tribulations life presents to people as they grow old. Over the past four years at Andover, I have had to deal with a number of these issues, perhaps on a smaller scale, which are comparable to situations from *Dance*.

One of the main themes Anthony Powell ties into his twelve volume sequence is the reconnection with friends of the past. He sets up characters to enter each other's lives, to lose touch for some reason or another, and then to reencounter one another somewhere further down the road. This raised a few very interesting questions for me. I wondered if I would continue to, by chance, bump into cronies from Andover for the rest of my life, just as Nicholas did? Would I be married to my high school sweetheart in 10 years? Would I be working for someone who, at one time during my Andover career, I considered to be inferior to me? While I have absolutely no way of predicting this, *A Dance to the Music of Time* brilliantly highlights the reconnection and reconciliation of friendships along many decades, and suggests that, perhaps, I too may continue to bump into faces of my past.

In addition to adding to my thirst for the next stage in life, *Dance* also inspired me to compare and contrast certain characters from the novel to people who have walked in, and possibly out, of my own life. As I completed each volume, I was careful to note any characters with whom I shared a particular connection, or whom I could compare to persons I have encountered along my own "dance to the music of time." This activity became especially entertaining for me at times. (For instance, if my roommate was being bothersome, I would tell her she was acting too much like Lady Widmerpool for me to handle. Boy, if she ever knew!)

After completing the novel, I decided that there was not one character whom I identified most with, but rather I found that I possessed certain aspects of many different characters. I found that this was also true when trying to compare friends to characters from the novel. Powell created his characters in *A Dance to the Music of Time* by incorporating several different personality traits from real life people he knew, but did not model any character on solely one of them.

Certain events from *A Dance to the Music of Time* are reminiscent of events which have occurred over the past four years at Andover. I am very pleased that I have had the privilege of taking this course all year. I have enjoyed drawing parallels between my life and the lives of various characters from the books and I have had a fun time making comparisons between characters and my own friends. I am glad that *A Dance to the Music of Time*'s ending has come simultaneously with the end of my Andover career.

I hope that, in the future, I am blessed with reconnections, similar to the ones Nick makes with people he knows throughout his life. My dance continues...

©Madeleine Fawcett, 2002

Lightning Source UK Ltd.
Milton Keynes UK
25 August 2009

143070UK00001B/25/P